WOMAN QUESTIONS

WOMAN QUESTIONS

Essays for a Materialist Feminism

Lise Vogel

Pluto  Press

LONDON

First published in the UK by Pluto Press
345 Archway Road, London N6 5AA

British Library Cataloguing in Publication Data
A catalogue record is available from the British Library

ISBN 0 7453 0675 6 hbk

Designed and produced for Pluto Press by
Chase Production Services, Chipping Norton, OX7 5QR
Printed in the EC by T J Press, Padstow, England

What will happen to all that beauty?

— James Baldwin,
The Fire Next Time (1963)

CONTENTS

SOURCES

Chapters 2–8 are reworkings of articles that originally appeared in the following publications. The author and publisher acknowledge, with thanks, permission to use them here.

Chapter 2: 'Questions on the Woman Question', *Monthly Review* 31, no. 2 (June 1979), 39–59.

Chapter 3: 'Socialist Feminism', *Encyclopedia of the American Left* (New York: Garland Publishing, 1990).

Chapter 4: 'Marxism and Feminism: Unhappy Marriage, Trial Separation, or Something Else?' in *Women and Revolution*, ed. Lydia Sargent (Boston, MA: South End Press, 1981/London: Pluto Press, 1982).

Chapter 5: Chapter 6 of *Marxism and the Oppression of Women: Toward a Unitary Theory* (New Brunswick, NJ: Rutgers University Press, 1983).

Chapter 6: 'On: "Women's Self-Organization"', *Monthly Review* 34, no. 11 (April 1983), 47–52.

Chapter 7: 'On: "Class Roots of Feminism"', *Monthly Review* 28, no. 9 (February 1977), 52–60.

Chapter 8: 'Telling Tales: Historians of Our Own Lives', *Journal of Women's History* 2 (Winter 1991), 89–101

ACKNOWLEDGMENTS

The support of colleagues and friends has been, as always, critical to my work on this book. I am especially indebted to the many who read the Introduction. If I have been able to overcome my qualms about the pitfalls of memory and the hazards of personal story-telling, it is in part due to their thoughtful comments and good conversation. I particularly thank Hester Eisenstein, Jack Hammond and Susan Reverby, who managed to maintain wisdom and judgment through as many as three or four versions. Numerous others also kindly took the time to read the manuscript, pushing me to explain better and say more. For their comments and encouragement I am deeply grateful to Renate Bridenthal, Leonard Gordon, Sue Houchins, Elizabeth James, Radhika Lal, Paul Montagna, Molly Nolan, Judith Rollins, Annette Rubinstein, Ellen Schrecker, Debra Schultz, Mary Tuominen, Carole Turbin, Deborah Valenze and Adele Vexler. I must also thank Chude Allen, Doug McAdam and Barbara Ellen Smith for keeping in contact over the years and for helping me reconnect with my time in the South.

Gripped by the fascination and, sometimes, terror of auto-biography, I turned also to the memories of others. My appreciation and love to family and friends who willingly discussed with me our shared histories – John and Gill Vogel, Beth and Ben Berkov, Michael and Anita Colloms, and Jake and Ruth Epstein. They will recognize, of course, that the interpretations I have drawn from our conversations about growing up among the Morells and the Vogels are mine alone. In her own way Betty Carter has also been a wonderful source of information; I am grateful to Ann and Carl Carter for making it possible for me to see her in recent years. I am indebted as well to several friends from the 1960s who graciously responded to my queries, direct as well as oblique, about matters perhaps long forgotten. My thanks to Barry Mazur, Jim Reiss, John Schrecker and Robert Weil for conversations about our pasts and about the present too. And a special thank you to Lillian Robinson, who not only considered my questions in lengthy detail but also went through the manuscript with her ever sharp and always witty pencil.

Rider University's readiness over the years to grant me fellowships and time has enabled me to bring many of the essays included here to completion. For its consistent backing of my research I am deeply grateful. During the last stages of manuscript preparation, the Laura C. Harris Distinguished Visiting Professorship at Denison University generously provided time and research support. I am particularly indebted to Denison's Sociology/Anthropology Department and Women's Studies Program for making my visit a happy and productive one. And a special thanks to Elaine Hensley, secretary of the Sociology/Anthropology Department, and to the staff at the Denison Library for helping me attend to many details. My gratitude goes also to the University Seminars at Columbia University for its assistance with the costs of preparing the manuscript for publication; several of the essays incorporate material first presented to the University Seminar on Women and Society.

At Pluto Press, Roger van Zwanenberg invited me to think about collecting my essays and Anne Beech shepherded the project through. My sincerest appreciation to them for their enthusiasm and care. Thanks too to Pluto Press for perspicacious copyediting and for translating my American into crossover English. Lastly, I was fortunate again to be able to rely on the skills of Jim O'Brien, who cares as much as I do about what it takes to produce a good index.

PREFACE

The essays in this book offer a perspective on the possibilities of women's liberation. I collect them here with several purposes in mind. The first is to provide an introduction to socialist feminism, the position within the modern women's movement from which I started. The second is to contribute to a rethinking of the history of the women's movement. And the third is to continue the discussion of the significance of a feminist agenda for social transformation.

Written between 1976 and 1994, these chapters come out of a particular history, which I explore in the Introduction. On the one hand, I review the development of modern feminism as part of the social ferment of the 1960s. On the other, I examine my own experience as a person who came to political and intellectual awareness during that decade. Telling this autobiographical portion of the story has sometimes seemed a peculiar exercise – a self-fictional act, to use Nancy Miller's term – and vulnerable to unfriendly reading. I offer this narrative nonetheless, for I find I am invested, as Judith Newton puts it, in placing my own version of the history on record.[1]

The essays are grouped in three sections. In the first, I address the relationship between the women's movement and the socialist legacy. In the second, I draw on my investigation of the Marxist theoretical tradition. In the third, I consider issues of difference, diversity and equality. Seeking to eliminate repetition and to clarify arguments, I have edited the texts extensively. I have not meant, however, to alter their original sense and flavor, even where my language now appears somewhat antiquated. To bridge the interruptions of time and shifting politics, I provide each chapter with its own introductory commentary.

Taken together, these essays reflect the position I have staked out since the 1970s within socialist-feminist thought, a position that, I think, resists easy categorization. Thus I reject additive solutions to the problem of theorizing gender, class and race, refuse to interpret Marxism as merely an economic theory, and insist that socialists and socialist feminists must take issues of equality seriously. By collecting these writings here I suggest, obviously, that socialist feminism is still pertinent today.

The title I have chosen for this book claims both a connection with and a critique of the socialist tradition. In the late 1960s, the socialist legacy on the 'woman question' was often a starting point for women's liberation theorists.[2] But we always had our own questions about the woman question and, in the end, we rejected much of the thinking associated with it. In returning to this formulation for my title, I mean to honor the contradictory origins of contemporary feminist thought in the socialism and socialist feminism of the 1970s and earlier.

Socialist feminists sought to replace the socialist tradition's theorizing about the woman question with a 'materialist' understanding of women's oppression. But it was never entirely clear what we meant by materialism. Wishing both to invoke Marxism and to maintain our distance, we deployed the term to signal the key role, mediated and determinant only in the last instance, of human labor and material processes – most especially those carried out primarily by women and previously invisible to theory.

The concept of materialism also functioned as a sort of flag, positioning socialist feminists within contemporary feminist discourse, on the one hand, and the left, on the other. Taking down the tattered banner of the woman question, we hoisted in its place the colors of materialist feminism.[3] I still walk happily beneath that sign (even as I think that what counts more than our flag is what happens on the ground). And I continue to ask woman questions and to demand in reply materialist-feminist answers.

Notes

1. Nancy Miller, *Getting Personal: Feminist Occasions and Other Autobiographical Acts* (New York: Routledge, 1991), xiii, 24; Judith Newton, *Starting Over: Feminism and the Politics of Cultural Critique* (Ann Arbor: University of Michigan Press, 1994), xvii.
2. For example, Shulamith Firestone, *The Dialectic of Sex: The Case for Feminist Revolution* (New York: Morrow, 1970); Kate Millett, *Sexual Politics* (New York: Doubleday, 1970); Miriam Schneir, ed., *Feminism in Our Time: The Essential Writings, World War II to the Present* (New York: Vintage Books, 1994), 103–48, 175–87, 201–12.
3. Efforts by literary critics to restrict the term materialist feminism to a trend within cultural studies seem to me too easy, as do attempts to demarcate a clear line between materialist-feminist and Marxist criticism. Both strategies evade difficult questions of politics, history and theory.

1 INTRODUCTION

The essays that follow bear witness to my engagement with feminism. Published over a period of nearly twenty years, their origins
lie in an earlier personal and political history. To set them in
context I must therefore go back further in time, and particularly
to the 1960s – the decade during which I, along with many other
Americans, found myself swept up in mass movements for social
change. These were the years that constituted the fertile mix from
which sprang the modern women's movement, and within it the
women's liberation activism in which I participated. It was during
these years as well that I became aware of myself as a political
and intellectual being.

The emergence and development of the modern US women's movement is a story whose tangled threads researchers are only now
beginning to unravel. [1] Organizationally and politically diverse,
'second-wave' feminism had its roots in women's increasing participation in the labor force after World War II. Its first demands, made
at the start of the 1960s, were for women's full inclusion in all
aspects of American society. This 'liberal feminism' located women's
oppression in the denial of rights and opportunities promised to all
by the liberal state and sought equality through legal remedies and
government action. Looking to the mainstream civil rights organizations for strategic and ideological inspiration, liberal feminists
worked vigorously to eliminate obstacles to women's self-development, social and economic participation, and citizenship. Liberal-
feminist organizations such as the National Organization for
Women (NOW) played a leading role in the removal of the legal
impediments still disadvantaging women in the 1960s and 1970s,
and they continue today to be in the forefront of the cause of
women.
  In the later 1960s, a different sort of second-wave feminism
appeared. Calling itself 'women's liberation', this movement aimed
to go beyond liberal feminism's interest in equality within the
existing system. In a period marked by worldwide political and

cultural upheaval, radical social transformation seemed to be on
the agenda and liberationists wanted to make sure it extended to
women. Like the student left, women's liberation had a penchant
for locally based organizing efforts and for theorizing. And like
the more grass-roots oriented sectors of the civil rights movement,
its vision of liberation was participatory and collectivist.

Women's liberationists were generally younger than liberal feminists and they had a wider view of the reach of feminism. Bursting
with energy and creativity, they discovered issues that at the time
seemed entirely new. Child care, housework, sexuality, women's
health, reproductive rights, workplace harassment, lesbianism, bat-
tering, incest and rape, for example, became the objects of their
sharp-tongued critique and activism. To mobilize women, women's
liberationists invented new methods of organization. Consciousness-raising, small groups and collective decision-making aimed
simultaneously at personal transformation and participation in
social change. Almost overnight, thousands of women organized
themselves into women's liberation groups across the US, engaging
in consciousness-raising and proclaiming an activist sisterhood.

Many participants in the women's liberation movement had been
involved in the civil rights movement and they often conceptualized
women's oppression as differentiated by race and class. Contrary to
later readings, the term sisterhood initially was used both to encompass all women and to acknowledge their diversity. The trinity of
race/class/gender that became the watchword of 1980s multiculturalism in fact had an early career in the women's liberation movement, which universalized women's experience yet also sought to
pay attention to the impact of class, race and national oppressions.
Popular pamphlets of the late 1960s and early 1970s described all
women as subordinated and simultaneously emphasized the special
oppression of women of color and working-class women. Anthologies of women's liberationist writing included explorations of the
specificity of race, class, age and sexuality in women's lives.[2] Nor
was the interest in diversity simply theoretical. Although generally
unable to attract many women of color or working-class women into
its organizations, the women's liberation movement directed its
efforts at what it understood to be the women most in need. Battered women's shelters, incest hot lines, rape crisis centers, women's
health clinics, workplace organizing campaigns and the like served a
range of poor and working-class women in local communities. Here
and there, women's liberation collectives composed exclusively of
working-class women formed. And a small but significant number of
radical women of color explored the possibility of being feminist
without denying race and class subordination.[3]

Within a few years, two trends consolidated within the women's liberation movement: radical feminism and socialist feminism. [4] In many ways, adherents of the two approaches followed similar paths, especially insofar as they undertook practical activity on behalf of women. Socialist feminists put more emphasis on class, work and family, while radical feminists focused more on sexuality, self-help and women's culture, but the overlap of concerns was broad. The differences between radical and socialist feminism emerged more sharply in the area of theory, which developed in close connection with women's liberation activism. Taking the form of papers, pamphlets and newspaper articles, women's liberation theory circulated rapidly through the expanding network of women's groups. It soon became clear that radical feminism and socialist feminism offered divergent analyses of the sources of female subordination and the nature of women's liberation.

Radical feminists argued that women's oppression derived from a transhistorical sexual conflict in which men had control over women's bodies, sexuality and reproductive processes. In this view, all men as a group held power over all women and sexual politics was key. Not lack of rights and opportunities but a structure radical feminists eventually named patriarchy was the obstacle to women's liberation. Race and class hierarchies were important, but sex oppression came first, historically and theoretically. Liberation required the overthrow of patriarchy and a radical revision of social organization and cultural practices. Autonomous women's communities and institutions would be the vehicle of social transformation.

Socialist feminists also analyzed women's subordination in radical terms, but we located it in the structural workings of society. In our argument, capitalism (or capitalist patriarchy, as many put it) not only exploited women on the job and in the household, it also oppressed them by means of a pervasive ideological and cultural domination. Working-class women and women of color bore a disproportionate burden of capitalist oppression. Women's liberation would therefore require a restructuring of society in terms of class and race as well as sex. Although socialists traditionally viewed feminism as divisive, we argued that attention to women's special situation would make the socialist movement stronger. Considering ourselves part of both the left and the women's movement, socialist feminists formed autonomous organizations and worked in coalition with radical and liberal feminists and with 'new left' and radical Black organizations.

The heterogeneity of second-wave feminism is today generally forgotten. In the impassioned activism and theorizing of the time, however, differences of perspective took sharp and consequential forms. Participants in the women's liberation movement scorned liberal-feminist organizations such as NOW for being insufficiently radical. We did not fully appreciate the importance of liberal feminism in establishing a framework within which our radicalism became thinkable and possible. And political differences within the women's liberation movement too often blocked us from seeing what we had in common as feminists.[5]

Rich in its diversity, feminist thought gained a special influence in academia during the 1970s. Following the path opened up by Black studies, women's studies courses and programs proliferated on US college campuses. Feminist journals and caucuses emerged in virtually every academic discipline. A new interdisciplinary feminist scholarship began to take shape. In these developments, women's liberationists played key roles. But where women's liberation writings had once circulated informally, triggering spirited discussion and bearing directly on practical efforts to change the lives of ordinary women, feminist thought now increasingly took the form of scholarly articles and books. Younger feminists only rarely experienced the intimate links between theory and radical activism that had fueled the movements of the 1960s and early 1970s. For many, feminist theory seemed to be a product wholly of and for the academy – an academy that was, moreover, hierarchically organized and in its upper reaches almost entirely white. Attending to issues of race and class became a more abstract endeavor, too often not even a secondary concern.

Meanwhile, the women's movement was being forced into a more defensive position. Conservatives attacked feminist successes in securing rights and opportunities for women, targeting access to abortion in particular. An ideological backlash stereotyped feminists as selfish careerists and demanded a return to 'traditional family values'. In the media-shaped imagery of the 1980s, the women's movement became an homogeneous white middle-class phenomenon, rendering socialist feminism, radical feminism and the feminism of women of color irrelevant. The movement's more oppositional strands thus became invisible to public retrospection.

Setbacks and ideological backlash, coupled with the passage of time, have obscured the radical character and considerable accomplishments of second-wave feminism. It is often forgotten that as recently as the late 1960s sex segregation went virtually unchallenged across all major social institutions, discrimination against women was legal, sexual harassment and domestic violence were widespread but unnamed, and independence was a difficult, even hazardous, path for women.[6] A quarter of a century later, economic

4

and legal practices as well as normative assumptions about women have radically changed, generally shifting in the direction of equality and individual autonomy. Yet women's lives remain tremendously difficult, constrained now by the pressures of the second shift, single parenthood, and persisting discrimination and domestic violence.[7]

A profound transformation of women's experience has taken place. But, as critics began to point out in the 1980s, the transformation is not entirely the work of feminism or unequivocally to the benefit of women. Even as women have gained access to a greater range of possibilities, many of the burdens of racism and the class system have increased. And in the 1990s, global restructuring is bringing new challenges: pervasive un- and underemployment, falling incomes, intensification of racial and ethnic conflict, the reemergence of openly white supremacist and antisemitic organizations, and, some argue, moral crisis. From the point of view of everyday life, the situation for most people, and especially for women, is bleak and the prospects perhaps worse.[8]

Given the degree of social distress across the globe, it is probably not surprising to find hints of a renewed interest in radical thought and action and their pertinence to women. Despite widespread declarations that socialism is dead, and with it Marxist thought, the evidence suggests otherwise. In the United States, for example, conferences on socialist scholarship draw crowds each year and publishers' lists suggest a continuing demand for radical research. New journals promise to reinvigorate Marxism and restore such concepts as class, materialism and dialectics. Several recent essay collections consider once again the connections between feminism, Marxism and socialism. Participants at a session of a major academic conference answer yes to the question 'Is Marxism Still a Useful Tool of Analysis for the History of Women?'[9] Perhaps more to the point as I write these words in early 1994: a peasant army captures four towns in Mexico, its ranks including, according to an early interview, many women soldiers. The guerrillas' demands? Democracy, land and socialism.[10] In short, worldwide upheaval seems to be posing anew the question of socialism. And reconsideration of the possibilities for socialist feminism is following apace.

The essays in this book reflect my involvement in the women's movement whose evolution I have just outlined. They reflect as well the distinctiveness of my own development. I want, therefore, to tell the reader something about the encounter of biography with history as I have experienced it. Although single stories can only gesture towards the complexities of the past, mapping some of my crossings with these years will illuminate the concerns distilled in the writings published here. What follows, then, is one account of my path, with emphasis on the 1960s and 1970s, the decades that shaped my intellectual and political formation and the particular way I embraced feminism.

Mine is in many ways a familiar story, well documented in the literature about 1960s activism. [11] At the beginning of the decade I was a student at Harvard University. Like many other white middle-class students at such institutions, I was stirred by the civil rights movement and spent some time in the South. In the late 1960s, along with other women veterans of civil rights activities, I moved enthusiastically into the socialist-feminist wing of the women's liberation movement. And as radicalism waned in the 1970s I entered an academic career, hoping to sustain my political commitments in the context of women's studies.

My story is also unfamiliar, for it is, after all, only mine. Its particularity in part stems from my family history as a 'red-diaper baby' – that is, as a child of parents involved in the 'old left' political parties of the 1930s and 1940s. It flows also from the talents, passions, peculiarities, strengths and anxieties I found in, and to some extent inherited from, the members of my family. I cannot, of course, disentangle the various sources of specificity from each other and from what I made of them. I can say that my memories of growing up are filled not with a sense of middle-class economic and emotional entitlement, but with feelings of contradiction, marginality and dread.

As I recall, two worries absorbed my parents in those years: money and McCarthyism. According to family lore, the two were connected. If economic success eluded my well-educated father, a doctor like his German-Jewish father before him, it was a consequence, the family said, of the political atmosphere. Never acknowledged but certainly a factor were the mysterious personal demons that haunted him, provoking floods of rage and bitter melancholy. Whatever the cause, he was unable to do what was necessary to establish a properly substantial medical practice. Finances always seemed precarious, and the anxiety my parents felt about their inability to meet certain standards of culture and taste exacerbated my own sense of uncertainty. My clothes and my hair, like our furniture and our drapes, could never measure up.

In addition to worrying about money, my parents worried about repression and witchhunts, for it was the McCarthy years and they had both been 'political' since the 1930s. My father volunteered twice to fight against fascism – first on the Republican side in the Spanish Civil War and then as an enlistee in the US army during

6

World War II. Although he faced the risks of armed conflict, it was actually my mother who was the more involved in left politics. Often active in local campaigns to combat one injustice or another, she was especially outraged at US racism. Brotherhood, respect, solidarity, freedom from want, loyalty to moral principle, a kind of humane self-development she thought possible only in a collectivist society – these were the ideals that inspired her. And where my father tended to lecture me and my younger brother about exploitation and class privilege, she explored with us the questions at stake in particular situations. In a different kind of society, she always insisted, more generous values and relationships would be able to flourish. It was also my mother who comforted me when school friends disappeared from my life – sometimes because their parents were deported as Communists and other times because their fathers disapproved of mine. Neither my mother nor my father ever talked about their organizational affiliations and I never asked. After all, every week my favorite radio drama told me to be on the lookout for dangerous subversives.

As a child in the New York City schools during those years, I was both embarrassed and proud to be different. And I was vaguely troubled that my mother's name was Ethel, for it seemed to tie me to that other Ethel who also was political, lived in New York and came from an immigrant Russian-Jewish background – and whose trial and execution by the state left her two small children motherless. I understood without quite knowing that, like Ethel Rosenberg, my mother was a Communist.

Not only the activist and party member, my mother was the intellectual in the family as well. Growing up in Brooklyn, she was one of seven children and the first in her family to go to college. I remember her as a lover of words and thought, always talking and reading about social issues, about literature, about the world. When we sat down at the kitchen table, politics, ideas and above all history sat down with us (to borrow an image from another daughter of the old left)[12] – and it was my brilliant mother who brought them there. From her persistent inquiry, I gathered that everything could be understood as configured in history's prism (or, in today's terms, socially constructed), and that the key to that understanding, and to social change, was one's grasp of how society works. Progress for humanity would come through collective action on the one hand, and from the wonderful productivity of science and technology on the other. Even as I absorbed these lessons I sought to strip them of their political implications, for I wanted to see my talents as strictly intellectual and artistic. It was not difficult to force compliance with this interpretation from the circle of warm-hearted women – my mother, her sisters and her female friends – who fussed over me, making much of my every creative effort. My life, I assumed quite early, would center on knowledge.

I also learned a kind of feminism from my family. It was made clear to me that women lack opportunities they deserve, that male chauvinism is wrong and must be challenged, and that I should think of myself as capable and independent. Planting seeds that barely sprouted, these teachings seemed to me abstract, even irrelevant. My mother, sadly, could not effectively apply them to her own life. With all her intelligence and political insight, she was frustrated by her lack of development. Often depressed, she felt especially helpless during the difficult years of the 1950s – a depression intensified, I suspect, by the contraction of left politics and aspirations.

When I arrived at Radcliffe College, the female appendage through which in those years women obtained a Harvard education, I was quite unprepared for what I encountered. Coming from the Bronx High School of Science, I was baffled by the affluence, the private-school backgrounds and the sense of entitlement of most other students. I had always felt different, singled out since childhood for my seriousness and my parents' politics. And, of course, for being female and craving a meaningful career that would engage my intelligence, creativity and social conscience. At Radcliffe, my sense of not belonging only intensified. Yet on another level I knew I did belong – hadn't Radcliffe admitted me and wasn't it deigning to allow me access to a Harvard education? I plunged forward in an earnest quest for knowledge, mostly unconscious of the myriad contradictions swirling through me. Full of ambition, I also assumed – at first without reflection and later with impotent indignation – that as a woman my professional options were limited.

I had decided in high school that my major would be mathematics. Believing this to be a science and science a way to contribute to society, I put aside as impractical my longstanding love of art and developing interest in art history. But as I moved into the more advanced courses in mathematics, I had difficulty doing the work. Deep down, I suspected that as a woman I was not mentally capable of becoming the brilliant mathematician of my ambitions. Worse, I didn't find mathematics as interesting as I had hoped it would be. Sensing my growing desperation, friends and teachers tried to help. My algebra professor urged me to persevere, his advice a melange of charm and condescension. I met with my distinguished tutor, a kindly European gentleman with a shy demeanor, but neither he nor I knew what to say. It never occurred to me that the discomfort doubtless caused by my presence in the all-male Harvard mathematics department could also be a factor in my difficulties.[13] Before long I restarted my search for meaningful work. Perhaps, I thought, I need something less abstract and with more human consequence. Exploring in turn several other science callings, I could find nothing that offered the intellectual elegance that had drawn me to mathematics. In anger, frustration and anxiety, I dropped out of college.

It took a two-year stint in Paris and much internal struggle to gain the courage to switch to art history. What drove my decision was my passion for the beauty I found in art and my desire to study its history. I also knew that graduate work in art history would bring me into close contact with the refugee scholars of the 1930s, personalities in whom I thought I recognized my own yearnings. Their remarkable erudition, speculative intelligence and deep humanism were connected, I assumed, to an heroic moral history. By their very existence they bound, in my imagination, the search for knowledge with the fight against evil. As for my own need to feel socially useful, I hoped I could find a way, despite the art world's elitism, to make art more accessible and widely appreciated. When I returned from Paris to complete my senior year at Radcliffe, I was confident I would be able to quench my thirst for knowledge and moral purpose with a doctorate in art history.

In the 1960s, then, I was in the Boston area, a graduate student in art history at Harvard. My courses, at once spellbinding and breathtakingly hard, consumed all my energies. My professors, less awesome and more American in daily interaction than I had expected, seemed to welcome my efforts. In return, I revered them for their marvelous wisdom and for what I perceived as their devotion to the pursuit of learning. I had found the great men at whose feet I wished to sit and, miraculously, they were paying attention to me.

Grateful as I was for my professors' support and encouragement, I nonetheless gained a well-deserved reputation for stubbornness. When a truth about art or a principle about intellectual endeavor seemed to me to be at stake, I would not step aside. I was of course critical of the conservatism and market orientation of my chosen field, but I assumed I could maneuver through them by force of intelligence, hard work and ethical concern. The subtleties of departmental and art-world politics were beyond me, as were the practicalities of preparing for an academic career. Even less could I see the sexual politics that pervaded and sometimes soured students' relations with each other and the faculty. My status as one of the favored ones in the department shielded me from many of the troubles other women students faced. For the gendered awkwardnesses I did encounter, I knew no words or concepts.

Happy to have discovered my vocation at last, I was oblivious to much around me and thought I was flourishing.[14] At the same time I knew that social questions were being posed with increasing urgency – civil rights, civil liberties, nuclear weapons, peace. An old high-school friend persuaded me to picket Woolworth's in solidarity with the Black student sit-ins then sweeping the Southern states. I joined a student peace organization, somehow taking a little time away from my absorption in my graduate work. Soon, people I knew were going South to work for civil rights with the Student Non-violent Coordinating Committee (SNCC).[15]

It is nearly impossible today to communicate the mood of the country in those years, shaken by a civil rights movement that attracted wide support as well as violent opposition. African-American communities and organizations were of course in the forefront of the campaigns and made the most sacrifices. But whites were involved as well, often with a deep personal commitment to the 'freedom struggle'. Coming from a variety of religious, moral and political positions, they followed the development of the civil rights movement and managed to hear the powerful messages it was sending – astonishing medleys of love, anger and resolve. And they discovered in themselves as white people a desire for justice and the strength to act against segregation and racism.

To young people observing from the North, SNCC's gutsy grass-roots organizing, its respect for local initiative and its vision of the beloved community sounded a special call. Against soul-shattering injustice SNCC offered resistance and determination, together with the hope that collective action could heal the historic injury of racial oppression. Freedom, justice, community, love – SNCC seemed to embody a vision of the struggle that embraced all. And its heroes were students like us.

Drawn though I was by the civil rights movement, it was not until 1964 that I managed finally to pull myself away from my hard-won dedication to my graduate work. In June I travelled to Mississippi as part of the SNCC-led initiative that sent Northern volunteers into Black communities to live and work with local activists. My project was in Shaw, a small town in Bolivar County in the Mississippi Delta. Like many women volunteers, I worked as a Freedom School teacher and helped on voter registration days. Towards the end of the summer I participated in the riskier work of canvassing door to door for the Freedom Vote registration – SNCC's attempt to force the national Democratic Party to acknowledge the South's abuse of democracy.[16] The following summer I returned to Mississippi. After an arrest and twelve days in the Jackson city jail, I moved back to Bolivar County to organize in Shelby and then to work alone in the rural area outside Rosedale. In August I joined a van of civil rights workers driving from Mississippi to Washington, DC, for a demonstration against the war in Vietnam. This was my first antiwar demonstration and it ended with my second arrest.

Although I remember very little of the day-to-day details, the two summers in Mississippi marked my development more powerfully than any other experience. In the tumult of the 1960s, however, I was not yet able to take stock of their particular impact on me. Like many others, I simply assumed disruption, rebellion and wrenching personal transformation to be the norm. Each September I returned North exhausted and disoriented, became upset at the contrast between the seeming normalcy of daily life around me and the dramatic freedom struggle I had left, and nonetheless immersed myself once again in art history. I went to demonstrations, sporadically attended meetings of the Students for a Democratic Society (SDS) and made some effort to participate in the alternative education movement But nothing seemed able to capture my enthusiasm or revive my sense of political agency.

As I shuttled back and forth between my various intellectual and political interests, I felt at times quite schizophrenic. Perhaps most bizarre were the months after my 1964 Mississippi summer, which I spent in Washington, DC, as a Junior Fellow at Dumbarton Oaks, a lavishly endowed research institute affiliated to Harvard. Coming from Mississippi, I was struck not just by the hierarchies that permeated the workings of the institute but by my colleagues' virtually unquestioning acceptance of them. White administrative and clerical staff serviced the Fellows' every academic need, even sending a van twice a day to the Library of Congress to fetch and return books. And Black women, warm and gracious and insistently subservient in the Southern manner, took care of all domestic tasks. Well before the actual appearance of the women's liberation movement, I somehow sensed the convergence of race, class and gender subordination. A beneficiary of the arrangements myself, I felt powerless to do anything. I particularly recall my horror and embarrassment when the women, mothers all, appeared early Christmas morning to make us breakfast.

Within a few years, I began the transition from graduate school to professional career. Under the rigorous yet always kindly guidance of my two advisors, both refugee scholars, I completed my dissertation, a study of a key monument of Roman Imperial art. Soon, I had not only a doctorate but also a book contract with

11

Harvard University Press and a position as an assistant professor of art history at Brown University, in Providence, RI, then among the most conservative of ivy league institutions. Simultaneously, I continued to seek meaningful political activity, but with little success. Wrestling with the different demands on my time and energies, and confused by my inability to commit myself to late-1960s politics, I grew increasingly disheartened.

Meanwhile, small groups of women activists throughout the US had already started to talk about women's liberation. A series of discussions in the Boston area led to the founding in 1968 of a women's liberation organization with radical politics.[17] Each Friday evening, no matter how exhausted I felt, I managed to get to the meetings held, at the Massachusetts Institute of Technology, of all places. With others whom I began to call sisters, I embarked on an exhilarating reevaluation of everything I thought I had known. We talked about our experiences as students, workers, girlfriends, wives and mothers. We considered what it meant to grow up in the US as a woman. Sharing stories of pain and even despair, we identified patterns and named our oppression. The personal, we suddenly realized, is inherently political, for it involves power and subordination. We became angry at men as a group and, more distressingly, at the men in our lives. At the same time, we learned to value women in new and exciting ways.

Analysis and activism could not be separated in our minds. We adopted new terms – for example, sexism and, later, socialist feminism – and explored their implications. We incorporated our deepening critique of patriarchy into our hopes for radical transformation. As members of our own autonomous movement, we supported the Black freedom struggle and participated in the antiwar movement. Our awareness of gender as a political issue energized us. We invented new forms of activism and established projects to bring the message of women's liberation to women throughout the region.

A powerful longing for freedom and community flooded through these first moments of women's liberation, offering, it seemed to me, a reprise of the vision already conjured in Mississippi. The notion of a women's liberation movement struck me with an intensity of feeling I could not resist. Almost as compelling was the movement's mix of analytical clarity, political savvy and feminist wit. And, of course, the stakes here were even closer to home. Women's liberation moved to the center of my politics. Rediscovering my capacity for activist commitment, I joined a consciousness-raising group, participated in local actions, helped to write and publish women's liberationist pamplets, worked with a tenant-organizing project in a white working-class neighborhood, and co-founded an organization linking American women's liberationists with their European counterparts.

As the women's liberation movement gathered momentum, my involvement in its activities seemed increasingly at variance with my life as an art historian. On the one hand, my research and teaching excited me, my monograph received good reviews and I was well positioned for the future in a career I had always wanted. On the other, I could not ignore the sexism and racism I noticed daily in the academic world or the signs of mounting political crisis. And unlike colleagues in more populous disciplines, as a radical with a feminist bent I was virtually alone in art history.

For a while I tried to bridge the distance between the women's liberation movement and my dedication to my field, but I could not find a way that felt comfortable. Naive about the difficulties of starting over yet again, I resigned from my position at Brown and, as it turned out, from many of the professional privileges offered by the elite career I had just begun. I began to freelance in and around the academic institutions of the Boston area, thrilled to be involved in the creation of what felt like a revolutionary new kind of learning and scholarship. At the Massachusetts College of Art and at Boston University I taught some of the first courses on women and art. In several articles I sketched the outlines of a feminist approach to art history, mindful, as a socialist feminist, of issues of race, class and power. [18] At the same time, I started to move away from the study of culture. I participated in a series of study groups, some focused on politics and theory, others among the earliest efforts to define a new women's history. I co-directed seminars on women and work and on Marxism for Goddard College's Cambridge-based alternative masters degree program. Publishing in both popular and professional formats, I explored my questions about the history of women workers and about the relation of Marxism and feminism. [19] Through these various contacts with radical intellectual practice at the edges of academia, my commitment to feminist scholarship deepened.

With time, my participation in alternative institutions became increasingly problematic, plagued by political as well as economic uncertainties. I decided to return to graduate school and entered the sociology program at Brandeis University outside Boston. Although I had already begun to publish in women's history, sociology drew me for its interest in the present and its apparent openness to interdisciplinary approaches. This time, I no longer expected to sit at the feet of great men. Still intellectually stubborn and relatively naive about academic politics, I understood better that a degree is a job credential.

At the beginning of the 1980s I was thus once again a professor, now living in New York City and teaching first-generation college business majors rather than ivy league liberal arts students. Like many women who were involved in second-wave feminism during its early years, I felt in myself a steadiness and self-confidence that I cannot imagine having attained without it. And it was no doubt the movement's vitality, however contradictory, throughout a time of increasing social and political reaction that sustained my own political nerve.

Retracing today the trajectory I followed in the 1960s and afterwards, I can see its contours more clearly, although the details remain blurred. I draw several conclusions. First is the centrality of my experience in Mississippi. As many former volunteers also comment, I got far more out of being in Mississippi than I ever was able to give back. SNCC's combination of grass-roots organizing, mass action and canny use of symbol formed my sense of what a democratic movement for social change could be. The local people's courage, generosity, warmth and wisdom provided an example of the possibilities of popular mobilization on behalf of oneself and one's community. My work in the Freedom School and voter registration and my two arrests and twelve days in jail showed me I could function in demanding circumstances. At the time, I often felt unsure and bewildered, but with hindsight I think my efforts were reasonably competent and caring. In the end I knew that I had participated in history, that what we did made a difference, and that I had been tried and not found wanting.[20] And I had been granted a rare and intoxicating glimpse of a community formed in justice and love.

Along with the vision of community came hard lessons about race, class and identity. As a white Northern student in the civil rights movement, I could not ignore my own positioning within the race and class system I sought to transform. Each day in Mississippi provided evidence of the life-shaping consequences of being perceived as white or Black, poor or middle-class. It was also clear that race identity was something usually imposed but sometimes chosen, for everywhere there were Blacks who could have passed as white. SNCC staffers and the local community constantly pointed out the myriad ways we as whites were participants in the racial stratification system. These teachings – sometimes delivered with a kindly goodwill and other times in anger – reinforced what I had learned at home: that race is a social construction and that whites brought up in the US can never escape society's instruction in racism.

My reading of W. E. B. DuBois, Martin Luther King, Ralph

14

Ellison, Lillian Smith, Frantz Fanon and, above all, James Baldwin and Malcolm X, taught me more about the intricate webs of racism. Seconding what was to be learned in Mississippi, these authors catalogued the oppression and exploitation of Blacks with painstaking precision. They explained as well the many ways race privilege was intrinsic to whites' experience and sense of ourselves. And they insisted that a racist society damages the souls and constricts the hearts of all who live within its borders.

The early civil rights movement promised, in other words, a healing that crossed racial boundaries. To white people – 'the slightly mad victims of their own brainwashing', as Baldwin described us,[21] – it offered clarity, demystification and, of all things, freedom. Our purpose in joining the movement was, in the first place, to help put a stop to the terrible harm done to Black Americans. But many of us also understood the campaign for civil rights as a battle in which we each had a personal stake. Thirty or forty years ago, in contrast to today, it seemed agonizingly clear that the fates of all Americans were tied – that none could be free so long as some were bound.

In my activism I understood myself not as a racially neutral benefactor or guilty white liberal, but as an already implicated participant in a society scarred by racism. Where whites now often construe antiracist activity as something one does for others, in the 1960s many believed it was also something one could do for oneself. A commonplace saying among progressive activists formulated the options in sharp terms: white people were either part of the problem or part of the solution. To be part of the solution meant, of course, acknowledging one's own racism and complicity but it also opened up a liberatory potential. Defying my rational understanding of the tenaciousness of racism, my desire to be part of the solution stemmed from a wild hope that I and the community could be made whole.[22]

Involvement in the civil rights movement had, in short, an inspiring and empowering effect on me and it deepened my understanding of how irrevocably I and others were stamped by assumptions about race. It also expanded my schematic grasp of the workings of social class. And where I had ignored the early stirrings of liberal feminism and refused to read Betty Friedan's *Feminine Mystique* because I thought it had nothing to do with me, I was able to hear some of what Lillian Smith, W.J. Cash, John Dollard and Calvin Hernton had to say about the special implications of being a woman.[23]

The two summers in Mississippi drew me into the movement's hopes and dreams, but they also generated a fierce pessimism.

Schooled by my political upbringing, I had gone South assuming that oppression was a permanent feature of US society, impossible to eradicate without a thoroughgoing social transformation. Paradoxically, I brought as well a quasi-liberal faith in the protective powers of the Bill of Rights and the US Constitution. Being in Mississippi sparked these abstract beliefs into life. The evil character of racism as a national cult became palpable, its structural pervasiveness overwhelming. The strategic importance of civil liberties acquired a tangible presence, key to daily survival. Caught between the possibility of significant reform and the impossibility of truly radical change, SNCC did what it could. And we volunteers, rarely able to appreciate the difficulties and tensions within the organization we so admired, followed, sometimes stumbling, along. By the time I left Mississippi, I had a distressingly clear grasp of how wily and relentless are the mechanisms of power.

In retrospect, I see myself in Mississippi as a not quite helpless participant in an apocalyptic clash. On one side were powerful social forces that would stop at nothing, even murder. On the other were the goodness and heroic mobilization, but also the fears and everyday pettinesses, of the local people. Between them stood the flimsy barrier of federal law and a fragile and often embattled SNCC. For me as for many of the volunteers, Mississippi became a moment, painfully brief and never to be retrieved, of social transformation and collective healing.

Feminism moved me in other ways. Most obviously, its focus on women meant that its concerns drew me more intimately than did the freedom struggle in the South. The women's liberation movement's battles were, in the most direct manner, my battles. In addition, my activity in the women's movement taught me strategic and organizational lessons I had not been able to learn during my brief time in the civil rights movement. I came to understand, as I had not in Mississippi, how difficult ongoing involvement in a complex and changing social movement can be.

My participation in the women's movement also had a lasting personal impact. Disheartened as I felt at the end of the 1960s, I often saw myself as alone in my concerns and ineffective as a political activist. It was the women's movement that enabled me to confront my discouragement and think about the various relationships between the personal and the political in my life. Eventually the movement provided the context in which I could recover my enthusiasm as a more or less confident maker, alongside others, of my way.

The women's movement was of particular importance to my intellectual development. As an art historian with radical politics,

I was torn in many directions during the 1960s. A portion of me loved art, another piece delighted in puzzling over history, objects, texts and interpretation, another struggled with a critique of the university and of 'high' culture, still another studied political economy and socialist theory, yet one more sought to be a radical teacher and activist. I was juggling these fragments in some frustration when the women's movement came along, with its remarkably creative collective intellectual ferment. By becoming involved, I was able eventually to discover a way to bring many of the pieces of my life together. Just as I had been gripped by puzzles in the history of art, I now found myself riveted by the movement's questioning of the relation between socialism and feminism. The effort to unravel this conundrum immersed me once again in history, texts and interpretation, but this time in closer connection with my politics and activism. My analytical talents and scholarly training could be melded, it seemed, with my interest in making a difference.

The greater sense of integration I found through the women's movement could not, however, incorporate my love of art and my enthusiasm for art history. These remain external to my current intellectual and political life. My years as an art historian provided bearings that remain pertinent, however. Most important was the time in graduate school at Harvard, which fulfilled my expectations that graduate work in art history would provide a rigorous intellectual training in contact with wonderfully erudite scholars. My entry into art history also took place during a moment of general intellectual and cultural ferment, epitomized for me in my reading of Thomas Kuhn's work on scientific revolution.[24] Those years in Cambridge and Paris stand out in my memory as remarkably fecund – filled with people seeking optimistically to transgress boundaries and to create new ways of looking, new fields of scholarship, new ways of being. It was perhaps only a step from the kind of speculative thinking I did as a novice art historian to that I did later as a feminist scholar.[25]

The political, personal and intellectual inspiration I discovered in the women's movement was transformative. During the first years, I imagined feminism had recaptured and extended the civil rights movement's liberatory thrust, and to some extent it had. But something seemed to be missing. Looking back now, I think that women's liberation felt different to me in part because it had a significantly more focused vision – less generous and more realistic than that of the early 1960s civil rights movement. Where SNCC's emblem had been a pair of clasped hands, black and white, feminism projected a staunch independence, foreshadowing, perhaps, the splintering effect of so-called identity politics. And where in Mississippi I knew transcendent moments in which Blacks and whites seemed truly to come together in struggle, in the women's movement I rarely had the sense that others might fight for liberation alongside us. For me, in other words, the freedom struggle reached across divisions with a dramatic and loving inclusiveness I missed in the all-female and mostly white Boston-area women's liberation movement. [26] The early civil rights movement constructed humankind as (to use contemporary terminology) diverse but universally deserving of respect, a construction that resonated in me as just. A decade later, we in the women's liberation movement could not create a community that transcended differences, much less prefigure a fully egalitarian society. In addition, I missed in the women's movement the freedom struggle's insistence that the larger community publicly acknowledge historic wounds and enter into a collective process of healing them.

The women's liberation movement gave me, in brief, a new kind of integrity as a person plus the strengthening sense of being part of a community I could count on. But it never cracked open my heart the way Mississippi did. It might just be that my civil rights activism was a short period of intense immersion, easy to romanticize. Or it could be that by the end of the 1960s I was old enough or cynical enough to understand the limits of radical social change in the US context. But I think rather that the feelings I have about civil rights and what happened in Mississippi are intrinsic to the specificity of the freedom struggle and of my involvement in it. In subsequent years the gap between the permanence of racism and the movement's vision of justice, community and love produced in me a kind of enraged mourning – a grief to which it is difficult to see an end.

The events and experiences described here have of course shaped my scholarly work. My political upbringing, my particular intellectual bent, my participation in the civil rights and women's liberation movements mark the essays that follow. The thread that for me most links them together is my interest in the contradictions of equality. Since the 1960s I have puzzled over the ways equality can be at once a critically important goal and an inadequate surrogate for social justice. Initially with respect to race and class, and then later also from the point of view of gender, I have wondered about the tensions between human heterogeneity and the notion of equality. If each of us has specificity with respect to a range of collectivities, and if that specificity is historically constructed and therefore inherently unstable, shifting and strategically malleable, what happens to universalism and democratic politics?

18

Current scholarly and political efforts to pay attention to diversity promise to address these questions, and I am enthusiastic about this work. Enthusiastic, but also cautious. Amazingly, from the point of view of the struggles of the 1960s, diversity has gained acceptance as both a topic for research and an ideal in the culture at large. While scholars in academe's highest towers write and teach about marginality, exclusion and the Other, corporate executives preach multiculturalism at home and abroad. I share a growing skepticism about the meaning of this affirmation of diversity, for it is unlikely the conventional order could have been subverted with such relative ease. [27] We can look for power to be at work here, busily attempting to coopt, for example through a discourse that frames diversity as cultural celebration. Where formerly we were expected to dissolve our specificity in the melting pot, now we are said to retain some hard core of cultural identity as a piece in the gorgeous mosaic. Either way – whether considered one ingredient among others in the social soup, or one shining chip among others in the social mosaic – the distinctiveness of our historically constituted positions is lost. An enthusiastic festival of difference thus deflects attention from power and the stubborn harshness of particular oppressions. Innocent of hierarchy, it masks collective oppression and translates easily into a politics of pluralism.

Yet, for all the disempowering manipulations surrounding discussions of diversity and debates about multiculturalism, the recognition that the United States is a many-peopled society is here to stay. Even as American politics plunge rightward at frightening speed, social life can never return to the notions of purity and separation that reigned throughout the 1960s, distancing unruly Others and corroding every interaction. Nor will constructions of gender go back to the normative dichotomies of the past, despite bold talk of family values. On these questions, at least, things have changed.

Such collective self-clarification seems to me an irreversible gain. It is a dividend paid, in however grudging and contradictory a fashion, on the activism of the 1960s. We are and always have been a mestiza society, a patchwork of borderlands, a frontier for women as well as men, and at last this claim is being admitted. When the news of the day – yet another massacre, war, famine or plague, or one more indecency of urban misery – threatens to spin my pessimism into despair, I try to call on my sense of that gain. Pale shadow, or perhaps fragile harbinger, of my vision of the just community as multivoiced and splendidly heterogeneous – it does not always reply.

I Socialism and Feminism

7. Socialism and Feminism

2 QUESTIONS ON THE WOMAN QUESTION

In this article, first published in 1979, I made a double argument. On the one hand, I affirmed the relevance of Marxism and the socialist legacy for the contemporary women's movement. On the other, I suggested that the socialist tradition on the so-called woman question was a muddle of conflicting views about family, work and equality. Theorists never clearly specified the scope of the issues, political agendas and ideological confusions got in the way, and the potential for Marxist theory to provide insight went largely untapped.

Sketching an argument I was later to elaborate in Marxism and the Oppression of Women *(1983), I proposed that the socialist tradition actually contained two distinct understandings of women's situation. One position, generally dominant in the left and among socialist feminists, identified the sex division of labor within families as the root of women's subordination. The other, implicit in* Capital, *sought to situate women's oppression within an understanding of the reproduction of labor power and capitalist social reproduction.[1] The unrecognized existence of these two incompatible analyses created confusion and hampered practical as well as theoretical efforts to confront issues of women's subordination.*

The position that emphasized social reproduction needed further development, I suggested, for it augured a materialist understanding of the situation of women with respect to both family and production. By contrast, strategic and theoretical incoherence marked the emphasis on sex divisions of labor so common in the women's movement and the left. Reflecting the popular notion that sex, class and race constitute discrete sources of oppression, the approach severed analysis of women's subordination from that of other sorts of oppression. I doubted that this construction of parallel systems, each generating its own independent social struggle, could bear the weight put on it. As a theorization, it pushed oppressed groups into a peculiar kind of moral competition outside the workings of the class system. As a guide for strategy, it implied organizational separatism, a hierarchy

23

of oppressions, and the contradictions of what later came to be called identity politics.

My critique, written in the political vernacular of the period, was sharp and its tone staunch but optimistic. My goal was to intervene. But I spoke into a silence between the left and the women's movement that, in the United States at least, could not be bridged.

The women's movement and the left confront an urgent political task: to develop a theory of women's oppression and women's liberation that is simultaneously Marxist and feminist. The problem is not new. The contemporary women's movement, now more than ten years old, has always included a strong trend, known as socialist feminism or Marxist feminism, that seeks to merge the two traditions.[2] Similarly, the left has in recent years been forced to face weaknesses in its own practice and theory, and has begun to look for better answers to what has generally been termed the woman question. Yet despite considerable searching and some floundering, neither merger nor answers has appeared.

The woman question hardly represents a novel social issue. From the start, capitalism shaped women's oppression and the division of labor between the sexes according to its own particular character, at the same time generating both a variety of feminist movements and a vision of women's liberation within the socialist movement. Nevertheless, more than a century of socialist as well as feminist practice has not, I would argue, armed us with adequate understanding of the issues involved in the liberation of women. In this article, I examine the theoretical and political terrain with a view to establishing both a clearer picture of the obstacles to progress in this area and a better path along which to move.

'Socialist feminism' and 'the woman question' are two labels that indicate the same thing: a commitment among socialists to doing something about women's oppression. The two labels represent, however, quite distinct traditions politically, theoretically and strategically. The woman question, a term whose origins go back several centuries, has long denoted the historic socialist concern for women's emancipation. Socialist feminism, by contrast, is a new term, introduced by socialists within the contemporary women's movement.

Politically, the socialist and the socialist-feminist movements face the difficult task of fighting for women without succumbing to either of two temptations. On the one hand, they must be on guard against bourgeois feminism – the struggle for equality

24

within the narrow bounds of capitalist society. On the other, they should not allow simplistic or economistic views of class struggle to subordinate the fight for women's liberation. To put the problem another way, socialists committed to women's liberation need to find an adequate way to link the feminist struggle to the long-term struggle for political power and social transformation.

At the theoretical level, the contemporary socialist-feminist movement has inspired an important effort to situate the issues of women's subordination and emancipation within a Marxist framework. This work often starts, however, from the position that Marxism is not only incomplete but incapable of internal development or expansion. Thus, it is claimed, Marxist theory must be transformed by means of the insights offered by feminist theory and practice. In short, a theoretical synthesis must take place between Marxism and feminism.

Attempts to perform this socialist-feminist synthesis have, nonetheless, fallen rather short of the goal. For example, Juliet Mitchell's article 'Women: The Longest Revolution' – pathbreaking at the time of its publication in 1966 – has its theoretical roots in a quite conventional brand of sociological functionalism, despite its author's Marxist intentions. Eli Zaretsky's 1973 popular essay on 'Capitalism, the Family, and Personal Life', widely reprinted as a representative socialist-feminist statement, locates the concerns of feminism strictly in the 'personal' sphere and skillfully evades questions of sex conflict and male power. More recently, Heidi Hartmann's and Amy Bridges's important paper on 'The Unhappy Marriage of Marxism and Feminism' has responded to the growing discouragement among some socialist feminists concerning the very possibility of fusing their feminist commitment with the socialist legacy.[3] These texts, all of which have had an impact on activists in the women's movement and on the left, stand as monuments to the inadequate state of our theoretical development on the issue of women's subordination and liberation.[4]

Efforts to develop an adequate theory have generally been marred by an assumption that the socialist tradition on the woman question is both monolithic and easily grasped. In reality, serious ambiguities and confusion have, from the start, characterized socialist theory and practice on issues relating to women. Most important, the woman question has never received the theoretical attention it requires, with the consequence that Marxist theory remains especially weak in this area. I would argue that we should return to the theoretical tradition denoted the woman question, but critically and with recognition of contributions from the modern women's movement. In general, I hold that we do not need some new theoretical synthesis between Marxism (or social-ism) and feminism. Rather, it is Marxist theory itself that must be developed.

The woman question has a long and relatively honorable history within the socialist movement. In principle, socialist theorists have always started from Marx's comment that in a given society, 'the degree of emancipation of woman is the natural measure of general emancipation'.[5] In practice, socialist and communist movements have sought – as best they could, and often with lapses, weaknesses and deviations – to involve women in social change and to raise the woman question.

But what does this peculiar woman question ask? And how is it to be answered? The notion has never been obvious. Ordinarily, the term acts as a rubric covering an assortment of important problems: women's oppression in general, the family, equal rights for women, women's differential participation in social labor and in other aspects of social life, relations between the sexes, personal and non-work relations of all sorts. For example, August Bebel, the prestigious leader of the German Social Democratic Party and pro-ponent of women's emancipation, argued in 1883 that

> the so-called 'Woman Question' ... concerns the position that woman should occupy in our social organism; how she may unfold her powers and faculties in all directions, to the end that she become a complete and useful member of human society, enjoying equal rights with all.

In the present, he observed, capitalist society stamps every facet of women's experience with oppression and inequality:

> The mass of the female sex suffers in two respects: On the one side woman suffers from economic and social dependence upon man. True enough, this dependence may be alleviated by for-mally placing her upon an equality before the law, and in point of rights; but the dependence is not removed. On the other side, woman suffers from the economic dependence that woman in general, the working-woman in particular, finds her-self in, along with the working-man.[6]

Equality and liberation are thus always class as well as individual issues. Bebel hastens to add that the 'solution of the Woman Ques-tion coincides completely with the solution of the Social Question', thereby putting the final resolution of the question into the distant future. Meanwhile, the working class constitutes women's natural strategic ally in the struggle. Moreover, Bebel suggests, participation in the revolutionary movement enables

> more favorable relations between husband and wife [to] spring up in the ranks of the working class in the measure that both realize they are tugging at the same rope, and there is but one means toward satisfactory conditions for themselves and their family – the radical reformation of society that shall make human beings of them all. [7]

Like most socialists, Bebel also associated the woman question with issues of sexuality, love and human feeling.

Lenin, speaking of the 'clear-cut theoretical basis' needed to build a powerful international women's movement, emphasized that 'without Marxist theory we cannot have proper practice'. [8] Nearly sixty years later, the left still faces the same problem. The woman question lingers as a tangled knot of disparate strands, while contemporary social practice requires that the strands be disentangled and the knot untied. More precisely, we must identify and specify theoretically the object or objects encompassed by the category of the woman question. Only then can we begin to answer it in a successful manner.

Of the many elements included in the woman question, the notion of the family possesses the greatest ideological and psychological power. For instance, it dominates most social theory, left as well as mainstream, which still posits a model of the family as an isolated static household consisting of a full-time and year-round wage-working husband, a permanently out-of-the-labor-force housewife and unspecified numbers of ageless children. Yet such a norm – and the interpersonal relations it suggests – has long been in contradiction to the simplest empirical evidence. Even within capitalist societies, household structure and family experience have a range of variability that has never conformed to the model. A wide spectrum of household and family arrangements, including some with no relationship whatsoever to biological reproduction, has always existed alongside the supposedly typical nuclear family household: single-parent families, three-generation households, families spread across more than one household, childless-couple households, single-person living arrangements, children-only institutions, and households and institutions composed of unrelated adults. In the United States, for example, the so-called nuclear family has been, statistically speaking, a minority type among households since at least 1940.

The assumption of one male wage-earner, working full-time and year-round, is perhaps more significant. But here, too, empirical evidence conflicts with the norm, particularly for working-class households, which have almost always depended on several earners, each normally experiencing spells of unemployment. In the past, sons and daughters represented the major second earners; today, wives increasingly enter the labor force. In the United States, for instance, roughly half the wives living in husband-wife households work; moreover, the trend is toward more wives working, full-time, and for more weeks in a given year.[9]

In the socialist tradition, the demand to defend the family, a formula whose content has never been adequately specified, is a recurring theme. At times the formula may have corresponded ideologically to the crucial requirement that the working class be permitted to reproduce itself under the best conditions possible – that is, that the processes involved in the reproduction of labor power constitute an essential aspect of the class struggle. Today, however, it resonates as a moralizing criticism of any deviation from an illusory norm. Moreover, the so-called defense of the family has always clashed awkwardly, both in theory and in practice, with socialist commitments to, on the one hand, women's full participation in social labor and political life; and, on the other, the abolition of the family as it exists in capitalist society. Socialists have too often missed the subtleties in Marx's observation that

> however terrible and disgusting the dissolution, under the capitalist system, of the old family ties may appear, nevertheless, modern industry, by assigning as it does an important part in the process of production, outside the domestic sphere, to women, to young persons, and to children of both sexes, creates a new economic foundation for a higher form of the family and of the relations between the sexes.[10]

In reality, the socialist movement wants to defend the working-class family. Often the formula takes this somewhat more precise wording, although its substance usually remains unclear and implicitly normative. The insistence on distinguishing the working-class family from the bourgeois family is, however, essentially correct, and in fact crucial. It signifies a recognition that the family is not an ahistorical universal but, on the contrary, an entity rooted in a specific society dominated by a given mode of production. While this insight has a long history within the Marxist tradition, a variety of obstacles has blocked its development. Marx and Engels used the concept of property to tie the bourgeois family to the operation of the capitalist mode of production. More generally, they attempted to derive the form of the ruling-class family in any social formation from that society's property relations. But they never developed an equally clear grasp of the working-class family as an element of the processes of social reproduction in capitalist society. Even less were they concerned with theoretically situating the family in subordinate classes in non-capitalist modes of production. At most, they identified families as sites of fundamental material processes, and argued that the abolition of 'the family as an economic unit of [capitalist] society' is a decisive condition for women's complete emancipation. [11]

Most subsequent treatments of the family and the woman question in the socialist movement functioned at a descriptive level. Thus the vision of a socialist future projected in Bebel's *Woman under Socialism* fueled the aspirations of millions of women and men around the world, but the book's theoretical contributions were minimal and its strategic imperatives vague.

These theoretical weaknesses have their roots in social practice. In the mid-nineteenth century, Marx and Engels saw women entering the wage-labor force under extremely unfavorable circumstances and drew the conclusion that the working-class family was already withering away. By the end of the century, however, the socialist movement envisioned the possibility of a stable domestic life for the working class, and began an ambiguous two-pronged campaign: first, against the double oppression of working-class women in wage labor and in the family; and second, for the defense of the working-class family. Twentieth-century socialists inherit, then, a muddled tradition which has never been able to situate, *theoretically*, family, class and mode of production in the context of the class struggle.

For example, Marxists studying contemporary capitalist societies have difficulty locating families, and individuals within them, from the point of view of class and class struggle. Some take the occupation of the (male) head of household as an index of class, and do not permit another household member's participation in the labor force to affect this family class position. [12] These procedures, which are those of mainstream sociology, render a working wife or child invisible. Moreover, they entirely neglect persons whose maintenance and reproduction take place at sites that do not have a conventionally family-like character. Other Marxist analysts focus on the individual worker, male or female, and develop criteria of class determination that are independent of family or household membership. [13] While this approach accords class position to working women, it fails to encompass the reality of family experience

29

and suggests, by omission, that nonworking wives and children, as well as various types of institutionalized persons, have no class existence. Similarly, many Marxists cannot distinguish between 'women workers' and 'working-class women', using the terms interchangeably. It may be that they take direct participation in wage labor as the sole means of class determination, in which case all who do not so participate become analytically invisible. Or they may consider the distinction between participation in wage labor and membership in the working-class household to be somehow unimportant. In any case, the theoretical situation is confused and requires clarification. [14] The most serious issue concerns the class determination of persons not directly involved in wage labor: for example, nonworking women, children and disabled, aged or institutionalized persons. Historically, the left has acted on the assumption that the members of a worker's household are themselves part of the working class. This intuition is essentially accurate, but it must be validated theoretically.

In sum, the family and the working-class family are unusually powerful ideological notions, both included within the tradition of discussion on the woman question. Because of their serious analytical consequences and psychological overtones, they require a thoroughgoing critique, leading to the establishment of scientific concepts.

The subject of women's work – more precisely, of the work that women do – constitutes another major strand in the knot of the woman question. Women's work in capitalist social formations includes both wage labor and unpaid work in the household. For good theoretical and historical reasons, the socialist movement has traditionally concentrated on women's wage labor. Engels provided the classic formulation when he argued that

> to emancipate woman and make her the equal of the man is and remains an impossibility so long as the woman is shut out from social productive labor and restricted to private domestic labor. The emancipation of woman will only be possible when woman can take part in production on a large, social scale, and domestic work no longer claims anything but an insignificant amount of her time. [15]

The development of capitalism in Russia, on the foundation of a brutally patriarchal feudal culture, enabled Lenin to offer a more specific analysis of the import of participation in social labor:

It must be stated that the drawing of women and juveniles into production is, at bottom, progressive. It is indisputable that the capitalist factory places these categories of the working population in particularly hard conditions ...; but endeavors completely to ban the work of women and juveniles in industry, or to maintain the patriarchal manner of life that ruled out such work, would be reactionary and utopian. By destroying the patriarchal isolation of these categories of the population who formerly never emerged from the narrow circle of domestic, family relationships, by drawing them into direct participation in social production, large-scale machine industry stimulates their development and increases their independence, in other words, creates conditions of life that are incomparably superior to the patriarchal immobility of pre-capitalist relations.[16]

With the victory of the revolution, Lenin pictured the contrast between wage labor and unpaid domestic work even more sharply. Again and again he emphasized that 'you cannot draw the masses into politics without drawing the women into politics as well', and pointed to the obstacle that 'domestic slavery' represented to women's full participation in social life.[17]

Despite archaisms and weaknesses – man as the norm, domestic work as the exclusive province of women, sex inequality within wage labor as a barely mentioned problem – these insights of Marx, Engels and Lenin are essential. Theoretically, however, they remain undeveloped.

In recent years, 'housework' has become a major analytical concern among socialist feminists and some Marxist theorists. The general problem is the relationship of unpaid domestic labor, including tasks of both daily maintenance and child care, to social reproduction. Discussion focuses on a variety of questions, as well as on the relative importance, or even legitimacy, of the questions themselves. Is housework productive, unproductive or a-productive labor? Is it a constant across classes? Does some form of housework, or private domestic labor, characterize all societies? Is domestic labor a form of production? A mode of production? A mode of reproduction? If domestic labor is some sort of mode of production, how does it articulate with other modes of production; for example, with the capitalist mode of production? Why does domestic labor generally fall to women? What is the class position of housewives? How best can these issues be addressed? Which among them should constitute the starting point?

The sudden urgency of the question of the theoretical status of domestic labor has its political root in the fact that women today take an increasingly active role in revolutionary struggles around the world. As problems arise in the course of facilitating this participation, the general relationship of feminist concerns to revolutionary transformation becomes a pressing matter. Thus the debates about housework respond to political realities, although they misjudge the conceptual scope of the problem. The essential issue is the process of the reproduction of labor power, taken as a whole.

Inequality and the importance of the struggle for equal rights constitute essential aspects of the woman question. The socialist movement has always sought, often without success, to distinguish its position on equal rights from that of bourgeois feminism. In Bebel's lofty formulation:

> The goal ... is not merely the realization of the equal rights of woman with man within present society, as is aimed at by the bourgeois woman emancipationists. It lies beyond – the removal of all impediments that make man dependent upon man; and, consequently, one sex upon the other. ... *There can be no emancipation of humanity without the social independence and equality of the sexes.*[18]

But goals for the future are articulated more easily than are the means to be used in the present. Moreover, the nature of women's inequality, and hence of the rights in question, need to be specified.

In general, socialists recognize that the equality promised by capitalism is primarily formal and individual. Legal equality claims a special place, but the bourgeois pledge to democratic rights extends to all aspects of human experience. The early feminist movement, faced with the magnitude and intensity of woman's civil subordination within capitalist society, concentrated on obtaining a basic equality before the law. By contrast, contemporary feminism tends to focus on more subtle levels of inequality. It not only attacks surviving legal obstacles, but shifts the emphasis to broader issues of social equality – that is, to what has come to be known as women's liberation. Whereas early capitalism had been able, through the promise of civil equality, to veil its inability to provide the conditions for substantive equality, contemporary imperialism cannot. Thus the issue of women's rights reveals its revolutionary edge more quickly than ever before.

Without underestimating the importance of the fight for the defense and extension of equal rights, the socialist movement argues that in capitalist society, built on a foundation of class exploitation, real social equality cannot be achieved. As Lenin put it, 'capitalism combines formal equality with economic and, consequently, social inequality'.[19] Why, then, do socialists insist on pursuing the struggle for democratic rights? Because it is a means of establishing and maintaining the best conditions within which to develop and carry out the class struggle, as well as an essential end in itself. Once again, Engels supplies the classic exposition:

> In the industrial world, the specific character of the economic oppression burdening the proletariat is visible in all its sharpness only when all special legal privileges of the capitalist class have been abolished and complete legal equality of both classes established. The democratic republic does not do away with the opposition of the two classes; on the contrary, it provides the clear field on which the fight can be fought out. And in the same way, the peculiar character of the supremacy of the husband over the wife in the modern family, the necessity of creating real social equality between them and the way to do it, will only be seen in the clear light of day when both possess legally complete equality of rights.

Unfortunately, Engels's formulation, an argument by analogy, opens the way to viewing sex and class as parallel issues. One need only add the issue of race to arrive at a quite common misconception that sex, class, and race constitute co-equal contradictions, arranged in a theoretically arbitrary moral hierarchy and accompanied by parallel social movements. Despite its attempt to describe the particular role of democratic rights in the struggle against capitalism, Engels's text in effect denies their special character.[20]

This preliminary attempt to untie the knot of the woman question and examine those strands that constitute its theoretical components provides a basis for understanding the theoretical and political confusion that has historically undermined attempts to resolve the woman question, as well as for delineating its current form.

Within the socialist tradition, two distinct and essentially contradictory approaches to the woman question have always coexisted, although the distinction has not been explicitly noted. An unspoken and unrecognized debate between the two alternatives has therefore haunted efforts to address a variety of major theoretical and practical questions concerning women's oppression and emancipation. The theoretical origins of this hidden debate go back to the works of Marx and Engels themselves, and it has taken concrete shape in the ambiguous theory and practice of later socialist and communist movements. The implicit controversy has recently reappeared, this time within the contemporary women's and socialist movements. Although the hundred-year legacy of ambiguity still hampers work on the woman question, social practice in the age of imperialism – in dominant capitalist as well as subordinate Third World countries, within liberation movements and in developing socialist nations – suggests that the conditions now exist for resolving it, both in theory and in practice.

For convenience, the two approaches can be labeled according to their identification of the source, or principal site, of women's oppression. On the one hand is the 'family argument': women are oppressed because of the family. On the other is the 'social production argument': women's oppression has its roots in women's place within social production. In the first view, women's situation within the family explains their exclusion, or partial exclusion through deformed participation, from social labor and political life. In the second, the differential location of women within social production lies at the heart of their oppression in the family as well as in other spheres. Each argument suggests its own analysis of the various elements that make up the theoretical core of the woman question: family, work and equal rights.

The family argument starts from what appears to be empirically obvious: the family, the oppression of women, and divisions of labor and authority according to sex. It treats these phenomena as analytically separable, at least in part, from the social relations of production in which they are embedded. Thus it identifies the family, and the sex division of labor within it, as the fundamental source of women's oppression, and then seeks to understand the origin and development of this correlation in history. To the extent that the family is tied to the mode of production dominant in a given society and varies according to class, these factors enter the discussion as essential, but more or less external, determinants.

The family argument constituted the theoretical underpinning of most nineteenth-century socialist considerations of the woman question. It pervades Bebel's *Woman under Socialism*, and dominates Engels's rather contradictory exposition in the *Origin of the Family, Private Property and the State*. Within the contemporary socialist-feminist movement, the family argument often appears in the context of attempts to develop a theory of patriarchy. Such a theory would account for the special character of women's oppression, most particularly in the family, without denying the class struggle. Just as Marxism has discovered the laws that govern social production and class struggle, so the theory of patriarchy will reveal the material mechanisms that underlie sex divisions of labor

34

and women's oppression. Or, as many have suggested – basing themselves on Engels's remark that 'the determining factor in history is, in the final instance, the production and reproduction of immediate life'[21] – Marxism explains the mode of production, while the theory of patriarchy will explain the mode of reproduction.

Whether or not explicitly proposing a theory of patriarchy, all versions of the family argument imply a certain parallelism between class and sex phenomena. Thus they project, more or less clearly, a series of counterposed pairs: production/reproduction; work/family; class exploitation/patriarchal oppression; public sphere/private domain; social productive labor/private domestic labor; class system/family system; ruling-class domination/male privilege; Marxist theory/theory of patriarchy. From these pairs it is but a step to a more serious conclusion. Logically, the family argument suggests that some systematic mechanism, peculiar to the family and distinct from the class struggle characterizing a given mode of production, constitutes the driving force behind women's oppression. In short, according to the theory implicit in the family argument, two equally powerful motors fuel the development of history: the class struggle and the sex struggle.

Finally, theories that project parallel struggles of different sectors – for example, class, sex and race – encounter serious problems when they attempt to analyze the relationships between the various struggles. Theoretically, parallel struggles can never really intersect. Instead, to use the analogy of parallel railroad tracks, they simply appear to meet in the far distance, while actually remaining rigidly separate. As a consequence, a socialist strategy that holds to the family argument has great difficulty relating the fight for women's liberation to the overall revolutionary struggle. Such a strategy either takes the form of a women's movement that must guard its own autonomy with the practical zeal appropriate to its theoretical stance; or it puts the woman question off to the revolutionary future, while current activity subordinates so-called women's issues to the class struggle, economistically conceived. To return to the image of the railroad tracks, the first approach recognizes the true parallelism of the tracks, their permanent separateness, but thereby becomes vulnerable to bourgeois feminist errors. By contrast, the second approach falls victim to the illusion of convergence at the revolutionary horizon, while collapsing the two tracks into one for the purposes of present action: on such a railroad, no truly revolutionary train can run.

The social production argument starts from the theoretical position that class struggle in the realm of social production represents the central dynamic of social development. In this view, the concept of social production refers to the entire process of the reproduction of the social conditions of production, comprising processes of exchange and consumption as well as of immediate production. Before discussing specific institutions – for example, the family – within a given society, the particular mode of production dominating that society must be identified. For class societies, the category of the family as such therefore has no real meaning; instead, families only exist within different classes. In dominant classes, the family usually acts as the carrier and transmitter of property, although it may also have other functions. In subordinate classes, the family usually structures the site at which labor power – the individual's capacity to work that existing social relations put at the disposal of the dominant class – is maintained and reproduced.

The maintenance and reproduction of labor power is indispensable for social reproduction, yet it takes place, as it were, at the margins of social production. Women in subordinate classes have historically been assigned major responsibility for the activities that ensure the maintenance and reproduction of labor power. Furthermore, women's place within the sex division of labor characterizing these activities both affects and is affected by their participation in social labor performed for the dominant class. In a given class society, the oppression of women in subordinate classes is rooted in their particular relationship to the processes of maintenance and reproduction of labor power, on the one hand, and to social labor on the other.

Activity at the margins of social production necessarily has certain implications for the agents involved. For example, the capitalist mode of production forces a rigorous separation, at the economic level, between most aspects of social production and what Marx called individual consumption – which includes the material processes of unpaid domestic labor. In a given capitalist social formation, individuals who find themselves totally or partially marginalized with respect to social production because of involvement in these processes occupy a specific location within the social division of labor, with specific political, ideological and psychological effects.

The social production argument does not take the family and the working-class family as givens, for they involve concepts that must be constructed within Marxist theory. This construction is part of the work of producing a scientific theory of the reproduction of labor power, a task that cannot be attempted here. Some of its characteristics are, however, already clear and can be schematically indicated. The family represents a concept that is specific with respect both to mode of production and to class. Thus the term's seemingly ahistorical classlessness in fact acts as an ideological mask to obscure the class struggle. For the capitalist mode of production, the notion of the working-class family actually refers to the site and agents of the process of reproduction of labor power as a commodity, carried out in a specific social formation. This formulation allows for the great variety of social structures that function as such sites. Moreover, the class place of family members who participate in wage labor provides the key to articulating the family with the class structure.[22] The actual class position and experience of individual family members in a specific conjuncture constitute, of course, another question. In particular, political, ideological and psychological factors play an especially important role for an individual family member – for example, a nonworking wife, an aged person, a school-age child – who does not participate directly in social labor.

The social production argument suggests that the essence of the so-called woman question in capitalist societies is twofold. In the first place, women inherit, from an historically preexisting sex division of labor, the major responsibility for the processes involved in individual consumption and the reproduction of labor power as a commodity. Therefore, much of their activity appears to be unpaid services performed for wage-earning men, giving rise to a serious potential for sexual antagonism. In the second place, women, like many other groups in capitalist society, lack full democratic rights, and their political struggle to acquire these rights provides another possible source of sex conflict. In sum, women's oppression in societies dominated by the capitalist mode of production has a dual origin in their particular situation with respect to social production and equal rights. Of the two, women's confinement to domestic labor represents the major barrier to their real liberation. As Lenin put it:

The female half of the human race is doubly oppressed under capitalism. The working woman and the peasant woman are oppressed by capital, but over and above that, even in the most democratic of the bourgeois republics, they remain, firstly, deprived of some rights because the law does not give them equality with men; and secondly – and this is the main thing – they remain in 'household bondage', they continue to be 'household slaves', for they are overburdened with the drudgery of the most squalid and backbreaking and stultifying toil in the kitchen and the individual household.[23]

37

For historical reasons, the social production argument is even less developed at the theoretical level than the family argument. Moreover, the socialist tradition has evolved a peculiar polarization between practice and theory on the woman question. Practice is generally based on a narrow misinterpretation of the social production argument, while theory relies on eclectic and confused versions of the family argument. Socialists have only rarely recognized the existence of these contradictions, much less attempted to resolve them. Yet it is the social production argument that accords most closely with Marx's analysis of the workings of the capitalist mode of production.

The family and the social production arguments have different political and strategic correlates. The question here is the relationship of the feminist struggle to the development of social revolution. With its implicit assumption of co-equal oppressions, the family argument logically supports a strategy of parallel movements: the women's movement, the Black movement, the trade union movement. While various agendas can be proposed to federate or integrate these struggles in the course of revolutionary development, the fundamental character of sex oppression would imply that autonomous women's caucuses should function permanently, as a matter of principle, at all organizational levels.

The social production argument takes class struggle to be central, which makes unity of the revolutionary force the major task. Trade unions, as well as mass organizations built around specific issues – women's oppression, Black oppression, support for anti-imperialist liberation movements and so forth – would always play a critical role, but their existence and character would be a matter of strategy and tactics, based on concrete investigation of particular situations. Within a revolutionary party, problems arising from the pervasive nature of sex oppression and male dominance would be addressed as serious questions of cadre development, political line and organizational strategy. Clearly, the social production argument accords with the general tradition of Marxism-Leninism, although a thorough and consistent practice on the woman question has not characterized Marxist-Leninist parties in the past.

The demarcation between the two arguments concerning the woman question has never been clearly drawn. In the present period, many women in North America and Europe identify with the socialist-feminist movement or stand apart, as independent socialists, from existing organizations, for want of a better alternative. At the same time, most Marxist-Leninist groups, racked by inexperience, contemptuous of the women's movement and fearing

38

bourgeois-feminist errors, simply attack socialist feminism without analyzing its content. For theoretical guidance, they rely on the confused tradition handed down from the international communist movement, endlessly repeating various formulations from Marx, Engels and Lenin, while ignoring contradictions and lacunae. Ultimately, however, the choice that confronts us all is that between much of what is now called socialist feminism and a developed Marxist position on women. Our responsibility, then, is to face this choice honestly. The stakes involved are nothing less than social revolution and the liberation of women.

3 SOCIALIST FEMINISM

This piece was originally published as an entry in the Encyclopedia of the American Left. *Writing it in 1989 gave me a chance to think about US socialist feminism in historical context. Against media images and the passage of time, I sought to present a more nuanced portrait.*

The inclusion of an article on socialist feminism in an encyclopedia could be taken as a turning point. In a variety of settings, efforts were being made to construct the women's movement as history. By the late 1980s I had already been invited to speak on the topic at several conferences. Now and then a graduate student or a documentary maker would call for information or to set up an interview. A researcher tried to persuade me to respond to his survey of 1964 Mississippi Summer Project volunteers. Scholarly articles and monographs on the 1960s and on the emergence of second-wave feminism appeared with increasing frequency. I found these developments disquieting. In a period of social reaction, they seemed somehow to be a statement that what had once been alive now had to be dissected. At my worst moments I quipped to friends that we were being transformed into objects of study.

In retrospect what most bothered me was not the distancing of my experience into history, but its disappearance. The popular reconstructions of the 1960s and 1970s made little sense to me. Where I remembered an exciting jumble of organizations and collectives working on behalf of women's liberation, the media described white middle-class wives and daughters seeking individual fulfillment. Collective struggle vanished from the screen, together with the voices of working-class women, women of color, lesbian women and, of course, socialist-feminist women. Media simplification was to be expected, rendering my students, for instance, entirely unaware of the complexity of those decades. But I was especially disheartened to see younger scholars and even former movement participants offering accounts that echoed the media representation of modern feminism as monolithic – middle-class, heterosexual, individualistic and relentlessly white. I wanted to set the record straight.

In the mid-1960s, women activists in the civil rights and new left movements began to apply radical visions of freedom and equality to their own lives. The women's liberation movement that resulted, passionate and iconoclastic, conceptualized feminism in ways that went well beyond earlier feminist movements. Participants developed diverse views of women's liberation, among them socialist feminism. By 1970, socialist feminism had consolidated into a distinct trend within the modern women's movement.

Socialist feminists hoped to meld a materialist analysis of class domination with the best insights of radical feminism – its searing critique of male domination, its insistence that the personal is political, its creative development of non-hierarchical structures, its strategy of organizational autonomy and its commitment to free sexual choice and expression. Their goal was a collectivist transformation of society that would be simultaneously feminist and socialist. Within the women's movement, socialist feminists sought to develop a feminist practice and theory that could address the needs of the majority of women – be they working-class, poor, Black, brown or red. Socialist feminists considered themselves part of the left as well as of the women's movement, and many were active in left organizations. Within the left, they proposed that progressive individuals and groups pay careful and consistent attention to the special issues of women. Socialist feminists thus attempted to chart a path linking the claims of two quite different social movements. Not surprisingly, they frequently found themselves condemned as 'bourgeois individualists' by leftists, and scorned as 'male-identified politicos' by radical feminists. Nonetheless, they persisted in their efforts to develop an approach that would integrate the aspirations of the women's liberation movement and the left.

Socialist feminists emphasized the qualitatively distinct character of the collective experience of diverse groups, and they sought to respect the specificity of each. In particular, they rejected the traditional liberal feminist goal of individual assimilation into the mainstream. They also rejected traditional left analyses that subsumed issues of racism and sexism within the class struggle, or postponed women's liberation to be dealt with after the socialist revolution when all problems would somehow be automatically resolved. The questions socialist feminism posed to and for the left thus converged, to some extent, with those long posed by the Black movement within the United States and by national liberation movements around the world.

Most American socialist feminists hardly differentiated between Marxist and non-Marxist socialisms, in this way reflecting the weakness of left traditions in the United States. As the socialist-feminist movement evolved, disagreements concerning the relevance and interpretation of Marx, Marxism and the left tradition arose, but it is nonetheless not possible to demarcate some Marxist-feminist trend distinct from socialist feminism. Socialist feminists generally agreed that Marx and Engels paid serious attention to the so-called woman question, and assumed that an historical and materialist approach was necessary. At the same time they argued that the socialist tradition did not provide adequate theoretical or historical accounts of women's situation, much less practical guidance in the struggle for women's liberation. They differed, often widely, on the interpretation of these inadequacies, as well as on just which of the tradition's elements remained useful and on how to develop more adequate analyses and practice.

Socialist feminism took a variety of organizational forms. Small socialist-feminist collectives worked with poor and working-class women in factories and communities, seeking to raise consciousness while fighting for maternity benefits and child care or staffing battered women's shelters. Socialist feminists joined or formed women's health collectives that critiqued profit-making health care and developed self-help alternatives. Consciousness-raising groups, which were a central focus of the women's liberation movement, provided an exhilarating opportunity for leftist women to think politically on their own. City-wide socialist-feminist women's unions initiated campaigns for reproductive rights and against sterilization abuse. A national network of study groups pledged to dissolve the tensions between its members' Marxism and their feminism. Many socialist feminists also participated in the broader women's and mass movements of the time; they became active in local feminist groupings, in national organizations such as the National Organization for Women (NOW), the National Abortion Rights Action League and the Coalition of Labor Union Women, and in antiwar, antinuclear, environmental, electoral and other progressive campaigns. In the legal and policy arenas, socialist-feminist lawyers and activists worked to develop strategies that would go beyond the narrow individualism of traditional liberal feminism. Socialist-feminist scholars played a leading role in the development of women's studies in colleges and universities.

Some socialist feminists chose to work within left organizations. One group, the New American Movement, described itself from the start as socialist-feminist, and others attempted to deal consistently with issues of women's liberation. But most left organizations retained a traditional skepticism toward feminism, even in its newly elaborated socialist-feminist variant. Left groups were especially nervous about socialist feminism's critique of relations in the so-

42

called private sphere, its views on the family, its commitment to the organizational autonomy of the women's movement, and its endorsement of gay rights and a freer sexuality. Feminists who were members of such organizations often paid the heavy price of isolation from the socialist-feminist community without being compensated by support for their efforts from within the group.

Socialist-feminist organizations were generally small and short-lived, never able to consolidate the resources and stability of mainstream feminist groups such as NOW. By the late 1970s, the double assault of economic recession and political reaction had taken its toll. Some socialist feminists concluded that their movement had died, but many argued that although weakened it survived in altered form. All agreed that the gap between socialist-feminist practical and theoretical activities had widened. Socialist-feminist activists were continuing to participate in women's organizations, progressive campaigns and the left, but now largely without the support of the vibrant socialist-feminist intellectual culture that had earlier been an integral element of socialist feminism as a movement. Socialist-feminist theorists, increasingly settled in academia, pursued research agendas that were less and less determined by practical questions of social change. New generations of feminists came of age who had never experienced the organic personal connections between activists and theorists which was an everyday experience in the women's liberation movement.

From the start, socialist feminists sought to develop a theoretical foundation that would underpin their myriad practical activities. First in the form of papers, pamphlets and articles in movement newspapers or magazines, then increasingly as books and scholarly articles, socialist-feminist theoretical work burgeoned. One of the main questions socialist-feminist theorists addressed concerned the sources of women's subordination. Women's activities in the family household constituted, they suggested, the material basis of female oppression. Early socialist-feminist theorists used traditional Marxist categories to examine this 'domestic labor'. What came to be called the domestic labor debate was heavily criticized, however, as narrow and abstruse. Many proposed that women's experience might better be understood through the concept of patriarchy, imported from radical feminism. By the late 1970s, the predominant view among socialist feminists was that women were trapped within two coordinate systems of oppression, capitalism and patriarchy. In turn, this approach was censured for its simplistic dualism, and for its tendency to leave the analysis of capitalism to an unreconstructed traditional Marxist analysis.

The attempt to generate an integrated Marxist-feminist

theoretical framework for the analysis of capitalist patriarchy produced a great deal of frustration among socialist feminists. American efforts to develop socialist-feminist theory were hampered by isolation from the renaissance of Marxist thought that had been flourishing in Europe since the early 1960s, and by a general impatience with theory. In addition, the repressive rightward political shifts of the post-Vietnam era quickly undercut the previous decade's radical optimism. In the more realistic mood of the late 1970s, socialist feminists recognized that the ambiguities of women's experience required a more subtle analytical approach. Many rejected the conceptual frameworks that had led to what they now saw as an 'unhappy marriage of Marxism and feminism'. They turned instead to historically rooted empirical studies, to more eclectic approaches to theory, or to new philosophical orientations that challenged conventional assumptions about the objectivity and certainty of knowledge. Those socialist feminists who retained the goal of developing a Marxist-feminist theoretical synthesis undertook the task with more sophisticated awareness of its multitiered complexity.

By the early 1980s, socialist feminists were addressing a broad range of concerns: the material basis for and history of women's subordination; the specificity of sexism as opposed to racism or class subordination; the diversity among women, flowing especially from differences of class, race and ethnicity, but also from distinctions of age, ability and sexual orientation; the relationship between Marxism and feminism; the role of families in societal reproduction; the place of women workers in the economy; the situation of women in socialist societies; the politics of women's liberation; the interplay of sexuality, consciousness and ideology; the construction, reproduction and representation of gendered subjectivity. In addition, numerous socialist feminists found themselves with fairly secure positions in academia, where their work adapted itself to disciplinary boundaries. Socialist-feminist scholars participated in the feminist critique of the traditional academic disciplines, and in the development of new perspectives and methods, often cutting across the disciplines.

Because socialist feminism was a movement committed to social transformation, research into the politics of women's liberation was especially significant. Socialist feminists analyzed the concept of equality, both examining its origins in liberal political theory and affirming its radical potential. They investigated women's activism in earlier social movements, thereby placing contemporary feminist politics in historical context. Socialist-feminist studies of women in Third World countries emphasized the dangers of projecting Western concepts of the politics of women's liberation onto societies with sharply distinct histories and realities. The question of women's liberation in socialist societies was a matter of great interest and debate among socialist feminists, for socialist societies provide an opportunity to examine the relationship between feminism and socialism as it develops in actual historical processes. Socialist feminists offered a diversity of views on both the obstacles to and the prospects for women's liberation in socialist societies.

Despite its commitment to a feminist analysis that includes all women, socialist feminism was a mostly white and predominantly middle-class movement. Black and other Third World women generally remained at a distance from organized feminism, even in its socialist-feminist variant, as did working-class and poor women. At the same time, a practical version of feminism took hold at the grass-roots level among women in poor, working-class, Black and Third World communities throughout the United States. Although often refusing to call themselves feminists, unprecedented numbers of these women, self-respecting and independent, became active on behalf of themselves and their communities. They joined unions, fought for day care, sued their employers for sex discrimination and sexual harassment, enrolled in college and formed such organizations as the Association of Black Single Mothers, Mothers for Adequate Welfare, Mothers of East Los Angeles and the National Congress of Neighborhood Women. Strong, motivated and persevering, such women embodied in their activism the socialist-feminist analysis of women's subordination as rooted in an integrated system of sex, class and race oppression.

In the 1980s, the grass-roots activism of poor, working-class, Black, and Third World women was complemented by the emergence of networks of progressive feminists of color committed to developing theoretical as well as practical work around their concerns. Moving somewhat independently of organized feminism, Black and Latina feminists established research centers, founded publications and became skilled activists within their professional associations. For example, the Center for Research on Women at Memphis State University has assembled a faculty of Black, Latina, Native American, Asian-American and white social scientists interested in women of color, poor women and women of the South. The Center supports collaborative research on the intersections of race, culture, gender and class; publishes newsletters, bibliographies and a working-paper series; runs speaker programs, curriculum workshops and summer training institutes; and maintains a computerized information clearing house.

Through their activities over more than two decades, socialist feminist organizations and individuals have had a profound and enduring influence. Within the left, questions of gender subordination are generally taken more seriously than in the past. Fewer left organizations dismiss socialist feminism as mere bourgeois individualism, although their assimilation of socialist-feminist analysis may be limited. Some left periodicals – for instance, *Radical America*, *Socialist Review*, *Radical History Review* and the *Review of Radical Political Economics* – assume socialist-feminist perspectives in their editorial policies and regularly publish important socialist-feminist analyses. Within the mainstream women's movement, issues of class and race are often addressed as a matter of course. NOW, for example, transcends its liberal individualist origins by conducting campaigns that oppose economic inequalities among women. Such national feminist publications as *Off Our Backs*, *New Directions for Women*, *Feminist Studies* and *Signs* frequently reflect socialist feminist politics. In sum, socialist feminist perspectives and concerns have spread well beyond their origins in the women's liberation movement. Socialist feminism has not only contributed importantly to efforts on behalf of all women, it has in many ways set the terms of a new feminist discourse.

II   Feminism and Marxist Theory

4 MARXISM AND FEMINISM: UNHAPPY MARRIAGE, TRIAL SEPARATION OR SOMETHING ELSE?

Socialist feminists started from the assumption that Marxism and feminism could be brought together. Within a few years, however, many agreed with economist Heidi Hartmann's depiction of the relationship as an unhappy marriage.[1] Hartmann argued that Marxism's sex-blind categories made it impossible to pose feminist questions, whether theoretical or political. Describing capitalism and patriarchy as separate systems, she endorsed a new kind of politics based on alliances between autonomous groups with different interests: 'We must have our own organizations and our own power base.'[2]

The image of an unhappy marriage had a powerful appeal for American feminists in the later 1970s. The economy seemed to be in permanent decline, the right was gathering strength for an assault and the left was becoming increasingly marginal. Practical political answers, especially concerning the importance of autonomous women's organizations, counted more than hopes about a theory that might meld feminism and Marxism.

In this essay, originally published in 1981 in a collection of responses to Hartmann's position, I rejected the dualism of the marriage metaphor as well as the widespread belief that a feminist divorce from Marxism was necessary. Although I acknowledged the failings of much of the socialist tradition – rigid, economistic, inattentive to differences of sex and race – I held to the possibility of developing a materialist theory and politics that would be stronger for being simultaneously feminist and Marxist. My argument rested on a critical reading of socialist-feminist theory.

49

In 1975 the first version of a paper entitled 'The Unhappy Marriage of Marxism and Feminism' began to circulate within the socialist-feminist wing of the North American women's movement. Both the essay's title and its argument found an enthusiastic welcome, setting the terms of a discussion that continues today. Authors Heidi Hartmann and Amy Bridges had grasped the current mood of the socialist-feminist movement and put it into words. In the wake of the events and activism of the late 1960s and early 1970s, socialist feminists were growing increasingly skeptical that socialist theory and practice could be transformed to accord with their vision of women's liberation. Along with Hartmann and Bridges, many had come to the conclusion that 'the "marriage" of Marxism and feminism has been like the marriage of husband and wife depicted in English common law: Marxism and feminism are one, and that one is Marxism'. And they agreed, furthermore, with the paper's strategic imperative that 'either we need a healthier marriage or we need a divorce'. [3]

Later versions of the essay, now sole-authored by Hartmann, added a hopeful subtitle: 'Towards a More Progressive Union'. Others have since informally embellished the imagery. In place of the unhappy marriage metaphor, a string of humorous if faintly bitter alternatives is offered: illicit tryst? teenage infatuation? May–December romance? puppy love? blind passion? platonic relationship? barren alliance? marriage of convenience? shotgun wedding? and so on. As the title of this essay indicates, I would describe the relationship as, in some sense, a trial separation. That is, to the extent that Marxism and feminism are distinct entities whose union may result in conflict as well as mutual support and healthy offspring, the socialist-feminist movement has generally maintained them in a state of trial separation. At bottom, however, the image of a marriage between autonomous persons is inadequate theoretically to the task of representing the relationship between Marxism and feminism. Here I agree with Rosalind Petchesky's suggestion that the goal is, rather, to 'dissolve the hyphen' between Marxism and feminism, and with Joan Kelly's projection of a 'doubled vision' that will move us toward a unified social outlook. [4]

In the following pages I trace the development of socialist-feminist theoretical work in order to assess its contributions. My discussion of the socialist-feminist literature constitutes an implicit critique of Hartmann's analysis of its insufficiency. Hartmann's pessimism rests on a conviction that Marxism must inevitably remain sex-blind, and that therefore it cannot produce an adequate understanding of women's situation. Hartmann suggests, furthermore, that socialist feminists have generally subordinated their feminism to their Marxism, and consequently have been unable to move beyond Marxism's presumed limitations. In opposition to Hartmann's reasoning, I maintain that the problem is neither with the narrowness of Marxist theory nor with socialist feminists' lack of political independence. Rather, socialist feminists have worked with a conception of Marxism that is itself inadequate and largely economistic. At the same time, they have remained relatively unaware of recent developments in Marxist theory, and of its potential application to the question of women's oppression.

In our critique of the socialist-feminist literature, Hartmann and I agree on many points. In my view, however, the problem at issue is not the quality of some marriage between Marxism and feminism, but the state of Marxism itself. As Hartmann observes:

> Many Marxists are satisfied with the traditional Marxist analysis of the woman question. They see class as the correct framework with which to understand women's position. Women should be understood as part of the working class; the working class's struggle against capitalism should take precedence over any conflict between men and women. Sex conflict must not be allowed to interfere with class solidarity. [5]

Like Hartmann, I strongly reject such assumptions about the adequacy of Marxist work on the so-called woman question, for they deny the specificity of women's oppression and subordinate it to an economistic view of the development of history. Unlike Hartmann, I hold that the problem of women's oppression can be addressed within the terms of Marxist theory. We do not need some new synthesis between Marxism or socialism, and feminism. Rather, it is Marxist theory itself that must be developed, and socialist practice that must be transformed.

Mitchell and the Structures of Women's Oppression

Initial efforts to develop a socialist-feminist theoretical perspective focused on the family unit and the labor of housework and child-rearing in contemporary capitalist societies. The opening argument, an article entitled 'Women: The Longest Revolution' by Juliet Mitchell, actually appeared well before the development of the socialist-feminist movement proper. First printed in 1966 in *New Left Review*, a British Marxist journal, Mitchell's piece began to circulate widely in the United States two years later. It rapidly

51

became a major theoretical influence on the emerging socialist-feminist trend within the women's liberation movement. The publication in 1971 of Mitchell's book, *Woman's Estate*, based on the earlier article, reinforced the impact of her ideas. [6]

Mitchell begins 'Women: The Longest Revolution' with a critique of the classical Marxist literature on the question of women. For Marx, Engels, Bebel and Lenin, women's liberation is 'a normative ideal, an adjunct to socialist theory, not structurally integrated into it'. More recently, de Beauvoir's *The Second Sex* is likewise limited by its attempt to meld 'idealist psychological explanation [with] an orthodox economist approach'. In general, the socialist tradition on women 'is predominantly economist in emphasis'.[7]

For Mitchell, the way out of this impasse is to differentiate woman's condition into four separate structures: production, reproduction, socialization and sexuality. Each structure develops separately and requires its own analysis. Together, they form the 'complex unity' of woman's position. Under production, Mitchell includes various activities external to what we might intuitively call the domestic or family sphere; for example, participation in wage labor in capitalist society. Conversely, the remaining three categories, oppressively united in the institution known as the family, encompass woman's existence outside of production, as wife and mother. Production, reproduction and socialization currently show little dynamism, but the structure of sexuality is undergoing severe strain. Sexuality thus represents the strategic weak link – that is, the structure most vulnerable to immediate attack.

While one structure may be the weak link, socialist strategy will have to address all four structures of woman's position in the long run. Mitchell therefore articulates a practical set of demands. In the area of wage labor, 'the most elementary demand is not the right to work or receive equal pay for work – the two traditional reformist demands – but *the right to equal work itself*'. With respect to the family, 'the revolutionary demand should be for the liberation of [its] functions from an oppressive monolithic fusion'.[8]

Questions about Mitchell's analysis of woman's situation arise in four areas. First, the discussion of the empirical state of the separate structures is extremely weak, a failure that has, or should have, consequences in the realm of strategy. To maintain that 'production, reproduction, and socialization are all more or less stationary in the West today in that they have not changed for three or more decades' grossly misrepresents not only postwar history but the evolution of twentieth-century capitalism. Moreover, as Mitchell herself sometimes recognizes, the contradictions produced by rapid movement in all four of her structures form the very context for the emergence of the women's liberation movement. A generally inadequate historical vision accompanies Mitchell's failure to identify contemporary changes in the structures, and her work reveals, overall, a certain disregard for concrete analysis.

Second, Mitchell's view of women's relationship to production is open to criticism. She presents production as a structure from which women have been barred since the beginning of class society. Even capitalism constitutes the family as 'a triptych of sexual, reproductive, and socializatory functions (the woman's world) embraced by production (the man's world)'.[9] In sum, Mitchell views production as an aspect of experience essentially external to women. Once again she misreads history, for women's participation in production has been a central element of many class societies, including capitalism. In addition, Mitchell implicitly devalues women's domestic labor, and gives it no clear theoretical status.

A third problem in Mitchell's analysis is her treatment of the family. While she mentions the family at every point, Mitchell denies the category 'family' any explicit theoretical presence. Its place is taken by the triptych of structures that make up woman's world: reproduction, socialization and sexuality. At the same time, the actual content of these three structures is arbitrary, and Mitchell fails to establish clear lines of demarcation between them. Women are seen as imprisoned in their 'confinement to a monolithic condensation of functions in a unity – the family', but that unity has itself no articulated analytical existence.[10]

Finally, Mitchell's manner of establishing a structural framework to analyze the problem of women's oppression requires critical examination. The four structures that make up the 'complex unity' of woman's position operate at a level of abstraction that renders social analysis almost impossible. They provide a universal grid on which women – and, implicitly, the family – can be located irrespective of mode of production or class position. Societal variation and class struggle appear, if at all, as afterthoughts rather than central determinants. Furthermore, the manner in which the four structures combine to produce a complex unity remains largely unspecified, abstract and ahistorical. As a result, Mitchell's theoretical approach resembles the functionalism of mainstream social science, which posits quite similar models of complex interaction between variables. Indeed, the content of her four structures derives from functionalist hypotheses, specifically those of George Murdock. Despite her staunchly Marxist intentions, Mitchell's theoretical perspective proves inadequate to sustain her analysis.[11]

Even with its problems, easier to recognize at a distance, Mitchell's 1966 article played an extremely positive role within the developing socialist-feminist movement. Its differentiation of the content of women's lives into constituent categories helped women's liberationists to articulate their experience and begin to act on it. Its perceptive overview of the classic Marxist literature on women provided a base from which to confront both mechanical versions of Marxism and the growing influence of radical feminism. Its insistence, within a Marxist framework, on the critical importance of social phenomena not easily characterized as economic anticipated the socialist-feminist critique of economic determinism. And the political intelligence of its specific strategic comments set a standard that remains a model. 'If socialism is to regain its status as *the* revolutionary politics', Mitchell concludes, 'it has to make good its practical sins of commission against women and its huge sin of omission – the absence of an adequate place for them in its theory'.[12] In the theoretical arena, Mitchell's central contribution was to legitimate a perspective that recognizes the ultimate primacy of economic phenomena, yet allows for the fact that other aspects of women's situation not only have importance but may play key roles at certain junctures.

Benston, Morton and Dalla Costa: A Materialist Foundation

By 1969, the North American women's liberation movement had reached a high point of activity, its militance complemented by a flourishing literature, both published and unpublished. In this atmosphere, two Canadians, Margaret Benston and Peggy Morton, circulated and then published important essays. Each piece offered an analysis in Marxist terms of the nature of women's unpaid work within the family household and discussed its relationship to existing social contradictions and the possibilities for change.[13]

Benston starts from the problem of specifying the root of women's secondary status in capitalist society. She maintains that this root is 'economic' or 'material', and can be located in women's unpaid domestic labor. Women undertake a great deal of economic activity – they cook meals, sew buttons on garments, do laundry, care for children and so forth – but the products and services that result from this work are consumed directly and never reach the marketplace. In Marxist terms, these products and services have use value but no exchange value. For Benston, then, women have a definite relationship to the means of production that is distinct from that of men. They are the 'group of people who are responsible for the production of simple use-values in those activities associated with the home and family'. As an economic unit, the family's primary function is not consumption, as was generally held at the time by feminists, but production. The family household is an essentially preindustrial and precapitalist 'production unit for housework and child-rearing', and women cannot be liberated as long as household labor remains private and technologically backward. Benston's strategic suggestions center on the need to convert work now done in the home into public production. That is, society must take steps to socialize housework and child care. In this way, Benston revives a traditional socialist theme, not as cliché but as forceful argument made in the context of a developing discussion within the contemporary women's movement. [14]

Peggy Morton's article, first published in 1970, builds on Benston's analysis of the family household as a materially rooted social unit in capitalist society. For Morton, Benston's discussion leaves open a number of questions. Do women form a class? Should women be organized only through their work in the household? How and why has the nature of the family as an economic institution in capitalist society changed? Morton sees the family 'as a unit whose function is the *maintenance of and reproduction of labor power*', meaning that 'the task of the family is to maintain the present work force and provide the next generation of workers, fitted with the skills and values necessary for them to be productive members of the work force'. [15] Using this approach, Morton is able to link the family to the workings of the capitalist mode of production and to focus on the contradictions experienced by working-class women within the family, in the labor force and between the two roles. In particular, she shows that as members of the reserve army of labor, women are central, not peripheral, to the economy, for they make possible the functioning of those manufacturing, service and state sectors in which low wages are a priority. While the strategic outlook in the several versions of Morton's paper bears only a loose relationship to its analysis, fluctuating from workers' control to revolutionary cadre building, her discussion of the contradictory tendencies in women's situation introduces a dynamic element that had been missing from Benston's approach.

Benston's and Morton's articles have a certain simplicity that even at the time invited criticism. In the bright glare of hindsight, their grasp of Marxist theory and their ability to develop an argument appear painfully limited. Benston's delineation of women's domestic labor as a remnant of precapitalist modes of production, which had somehow survived into the capitalist present, cannot be sustained theoretically. [16] Morton's position, while analytically more precise, glosses over the question of the special oppression of all women as a group, and threatens to convert the issue of women's oppression into a purely working-class concern.

Benston and Morton established the material character of women's unpaid domestic labor in the family household. Each offered an analysis of the way this labor functioned as the material basis for the many contradictions in women's experience in capitalist society. Morton, in addition, formulated the issues in terms of a concept of the reproduction of labor power and emphasized the specific nature of contradictions within the working class. These theoretical insights had a lasting impact on subsequent socialist-feminist work and remain an important contribution. Moreover, they definitively shifted the framework for discussion of women's oppression. Where Mitchell had analyzed women's situation in terms of roles, functions and structures, Benston and Morton focused on the issue of women's unpaid labor in the household and its relationship to the reproduction of labor power. In this sense, they rooted the problem of women's oppression in the theoretical terrain of materialism.

An article by Mariarosa Dalla Costa, published simultaneously in Italy and the United States in 1972, took the argument several steps further. [17] Agreeing that women constitute a distinct group whose oppression is based on the material character of unpaid household labor, Dalla Costa maintains that on a world level all women are housewives. Whether or not a woman works outside the home, or

> it is precisely what is particular to domestic work, not only measured as number of hours and nature of work, but as quality of life and quality of relationships which it generates, that determines a woman's place wherever she is and to whichever class she belongs. [18]

At the same time, Dalla Costa concentrates her attention on the working-class housewife, whom she sees as indispensable to capitalist production.

As housewives, working-class women find themselves excluded from capitalist production, isolated in routines of domestic labor that have the technological character of precapitalist labor processes. Dalla Costa disputes the notion that these housewives are mere suppliers of use values in the home. Polemicizing against both traditional left views and the literature of the women's movement, she argues that housework only appears to be a personal service outside the arena of capitalist production. In reality, it produces not just use values for direct consumption in the family, but the essential commodity labor power – the capacity of a worker to work. Indeed, she claims, housewives are exploited 'productive workers' in the strict Marxist sense, for they produce surplus value. Appropriation of this surplus value is accomplished by the capitalist's payment of a wage to the working-class husband, who thereby becomes the instrument of woman's exploitation. The survival of the working class depends on the working-class family

> but *at the woman's expense against the class itself.* The woman is the slave of a wage slave, and her slavery ensures the slavery of her man .... And that is why the struggle of the woman of the working class against the family is crucial. [19]

Because working-class housewives are productive laborers who are peculiarly excluded from the sphere of capitalist production, demystification of domestic work as a 'masked form of productive labor' becomes a central task. Dalla Costa proposes two major strategic alternatives. First, socialize the struggle – not the work – of the isolated domestic laborer by mobilizing working-class housewives around community issues, the wagelessness of housework, the denial of sexuality, the separation of family from outside world and the like. Second, reject work altogether. In opposition to the left's traditional approval of women's participation in social labor, Dalla Costa maintains that the modern women's movement constitutes a rejection of work. Women have worked enough, and they must 'refuse the myth of liberation through work'. [20]

The polemical energy and political range of Dalla Costa's article had a substantial impact on the women's movement on both sides of the Atlantic. Unlike Benston, Morton and other North American activists, Dalla Costa seemed to have a sophisticated grasp of Marxist theory and socialist politics. Her arguments and strategic proposals struck a responsive chord in a movement already committed to viewing women's oppression mainly in terms of their family situation. Few noticed that Dalla Costa, like Morton, talked only of the working class, and never specified the relationship between the oppression of working-class housewives and that of all women. What was most important was that Dalla Costa, even more than Benston and Morton, seemed to have situated the question of women's oppression within an analysis of the role of their unpaid domestic labor in the reproduction of capitalist social relations. Moreover, since her article functioned as the theoretical foundation for a small but aggressive movement to demand wages for housework, which flourished briefly in the early 1970s, it acquired an overtly political role denied to most women's liberation theoretical efforts.

The Domestic Labor Debate

Dalla Costa's insistence that 'housework as work is productive in the Marxian sense, that is, is producing surplus value' intensified a controversy already simmering within the socialist-feminist movement. The discussion, which became known as the domestic labor debate, revolved around the theoretical status of women's unpaid domestic work and its product. Published contributions, usually appearing in British or North American left journals, established their particular positions by means of intricate arguments in Marxist economic theory – abstract, hard to follow and, in the atmosphere of the period, seemingly remote from practical application. With some justification, many in the women's movement regarded the debate as an obscure exercise in Marxist pedantry. Yet critical issues were at stake, even if they generally went unrecognized.

In the first place, the domestic labor debate attempted to put into theoretical context the contemporary feminist insight that childbearing, child care and housework are material activities resulting in products, thus pointing to a materialist analysis of the basis for women's oppression. At the same time, the debate focused attention on the issues of women's position as housewives and of domestic labor's contribution to the reproduction of social relations. Various interpretations corresponded, more or less closely, to different political and strategic perspectives on the relationship of women's oppression to class exploitation and to revolutionary struggle, although theorists rarely stated these implications clearly. Finally, and perhaps most consequential for the development of theory, the domestic labor debate employed categories drawn from *Capital*, thereby displaying confidence that women's oppression could be analyzed within a Marxist framework.

At issue in the domestic labor debate was the problem of how commodity labor power is produced and reproduced in capitalist societies. Differences arose over the precise meaning and application of Marxist categories in carrying out an analysis of this problem. In particular, discussion centered on the nature of the product of domestic labor, on its theoretical status as productive or unproductive labor, and on its relationship to the wage and to work done for wages.

Ten years after the domestic labor debate began, certain questions appeared to be settled. As it turned out, it was relatively easy to demonstrate theoretically that domestic labor in capitalist societies does not take the social form of value-producing labor.[21]

Benston's original insight that domestic labor produces use values for direct consumption had been essentially correct. Domestic labor cannot be either productive or unproductive and women are not exploited as domestic laborers. At the same time, domestic labor is indispensable for the reproduction of capitalist social relations. Just what domestic labor is, rather than what it is not, remained a problem only superficially addressed by participants in the domestic labor debate. Some suggested it constitutes a separate mode of production, outside the capitalist mode of production but subordinate to it. Others implied domestic labor is simply a special form of work within the capitalist mode of production. Most left the question unanswered. The problem of specifying the character of domestic labor, and issues concerning the wage and women's wage work, now represent the central concerns of most theorists working with Marxist economic categories. As for politics and strategy, few today would use their analyses of the material foundation for women's oppression to draw easy conclusions about the role of women in revolutionary struggle.

Benston, Morton, Dalla Costa and the participants in the domestic labor debate set an important agenda for the study of women's position as housewives and the role of domestic labor in the reproduction of social relations. Their work proceeded, however, within severe limits which were not clearly identified. In the first place, they focused mainly on the capitalist mode of production. Second, they concentrated almost exclusively on domestic labor and women's oppression in the working class. Third, they generally restricted their analysis to the economic level. Fourth, they tended to identify domestic labor with housework and child care, leaving the status of childbearing undefined. Some of these limitations might have been defended as necessary steps in the development of a theoretical argument, but they rarely were. Although the discussion of domestic labor had been launched in response to the need for a materialist theory of women's oppression, its promise remained unfulfilled.

In any case, by the mid-1970s socialist-feminist theorists were turning their attention to other questions. For example, the domestic labor debate shed little light on the problem of whether housework is analytically the same in different classes within capitalist society, and even less on the theoretical status of domestic labor in noncapitalist societies. Socialist feminists also turned their attention to the childbearing and child-rearing components of domestic labor, and investigated the problem of why domestic labor generally falls to women. Since women's oppression is not specific to capitalist societies, furthermore, many wondered how to reconcile its particular contemporary character with the fact that women have been subordinated for thousands of years. Similarly, they asked whether women are liberated in socialist countries; and if not, what obstacles hold them back. Finally, the relationship between the material processes of domestic labor and the range of phenomena that make up women's oppression, especially those of an ideological and psychological nature, became a key issue. In general, these questions spoke more directly than the issues of the domestic labor debate to the experience and political tasks of activists in the women's movement, and they quickly became the focus of socialist-feminist theorizing.

Patriarchy and the Mode of Reproduction

While Juliet Mitchell had advised that 'we should ask the feminist questions, but try to come up with some Marxist answers', many socialist feminists soon disagreed. [22] They argued that the quest for Marxist answers led down a blind alley, where the feminist struggle became submerged in the socialist struggle against capitalism. Marxist theory, they believed, was incapable of incorporating the phenomenon of sex differences. To move forward, socialist feminism had to take on the task of constructing an alternative framework. Thus began the trial separation of Marxism and feminism.

Socialist feminists turned first to the radical feminism of the late 1960s for concepts that could address the depth and pervasiveness of women's oppression in all societies. Radical feminists typically considered male supremacy and the struggle between the sexes to be universal, constituting, indeed, the essential dynamic underlying all social development. At the same time, some radical feminist writings seemed to be extensions or deepenings of the insights offered by Marx and Engels. Shulamith Firestone's *Dialectic of Sex*, for instance, claimed to go beyond the merely economic level addressed by Marx and Engels in order to uncover the more fundamental problem of sex oppression. In proposing a dialectic of sex, Firestone claimed

> to take the class analysis one step further to its roots in the biological division of the sexes. We have not thrown out the insights of the socialists; on the contrary, radical feminism can enlarge their analysis, granting it an even deeper basis in objective conditions and thereby explaining many of its insolubles.

Similarly, Kate Millett's *Sexual Politics* acknowledged Engels as a major theorist, although her presentation of Engels's work transformed it almost beyond recognition into a subordinate contribution to what she called the sexual revolution. For Millett, the sexual revolution requires not only an understanding of sexual politics but the development of a comprehensive theory of patriarchy. [23]

Firestone's and Millett's books, both published in 1970, had a tremendous impact on the emerging socialist-feminist trend within the women's movement. Their focus on sexuality, on psychological and ideological phenomena, and on the stubborn persistence of social practices oppressive to women struck a responsive chord. The concept of patriarchy entered socialist-feminist discourse virtually without objection. Those few critiques framed within a more orthodox Marxist perspective, such as Juliet Mitchell's, went unheard. Although acknowledging the limitations of radical feminism, many socialist feminists, particularly in the United States, simply assumed, as Zillah Eisenstein put it, that

the synthesis of radical feminism and Marxist analysis is a necessary first step in formulating a cohesive socialist-feminist political theory, one that does not merely add together these two theories of power but sees them as interrelated through the sexual division of labor. [24]

From this perspective, the problem was not to figure out how to use Marxist categories to build a theoretical framework for the analysis of women's oppression. Like the radical feminists, these socialist feminists took Marxism more or less as a given and did not seek to elaborate or deepen it.

The task, then, was to develop the synthesis that is socialist feminism. To accomplish this task, socialist feminists explored two related concepts: patriarchy and reproduction. The notion of patriarchy, taken over from radical feminism, required appropriate transformation. Millett had used the term to indicate a universal system of political, economic, ideological and, above all, psychological structures through which men subordinate women. Socialist feminists had to develop a concept of patriarchy capable of being linked with the theory of class struggle, which posits each mode of production as a specific system of structures through which one class exploits and subordinates another.

Socialist-feminist theorists were not in agreement on the meaning of the concept patriarchy. For some, it represented a primarily ideological force or system. Others argued that it has a major material foundation in men's ability to control women's labor, access to resources and sexuality. 'Patriarchal authority', wrote Sheila Rowbotham, for example, 'is based on male control over the woman's productive capacity, and over her person'. Different approaches also emerged to the problems of the origin of divisions of labor by sex, and of the relationship between patriarchy and the workings of a particular mode of production.[25]

The concept of reproduction was invoked as a means of tying women's oppression to an understanding of production and the class struggle. Socialist-feminist theorists analyzed processes of reproduction as comparable to, but relatively autonomous from, the production that characterizes a given society. Often they talked in terms of a mode of reproduction, analogous to the mode of production. As with the concept of patriarchy, there was little agreement on the substantive meaning of the term reproduction. Some simply identified reproduction with what appear to be the obvious functions of the family. Several participants in the domestic labor debate postulated the existence of a 'housework' or 'family' mode of production alongside the capitalist mode of production, but subordinate to it. The concept of a mode of reproduction converged, moreover, with suggestions by Marxist anthropologists that families act as a perpetual source of cheap labor power in both Third World and advanced capitalist countries. A similar concept of the mode of reproduction was implicit in the work of socialist feminists who studied the relationship between imperialism and the family.[26]

Recent socialist-feminist discussion has challenged the use of the notions of patriarchy and reproduction, arguing that existing theoretical efforts have failed to develop satisfactory ways of conceptualizing either. In the first place, neither patriarchy nor reproduction has been defined with any consistency. The concept of patriarchy often remains embedded in its radical feminist origins as an essentially ideological and psychological system. Where it is used in a more materialist sense, it has not been adequately integrated into a Marxist account of productive relations. Socialist-feminist application of the concept of reproduction has also been imprecise, referring variously to reproduction of the conditions of production, reproduction of the labor force, and human or biological reproduction.[27]

A second theme in recent critiques is the problem of dualism.[28] Again and again, theorists using the concepts of patriarchy and reproduction analyze women's oppression in terms of two separate systems – for example, capitalism and patriarchy, the mode of production and the mode of reproduction, the class system and the gender system. These dual-systems theories, as Iris Young calls them, fail to relate the systems in a coherent nonmechanical way, thus producing a mysterious coexistence of disjunct explanations of social development. The duality generally recapitulates the opposition between feminism and Marxism that socialist-feminist theory had attempted to transcend.

Furthermore, the problem is not just dualism. Socialist-feminist theory has focused on the relationship between feminism and socialism, and between sex and class oppression, largely to the exclusion of issues of racial or national oppression. At most, sex, race and class are described as comparable sources of oppression, whose parallel manifestations harm their victims more or less equally. Strategically, socialist feminists call for sisterhood and a women's movement that unites women from all sectors of society. Nonetheless, their sisters of color often voice distrust of the contemporary women's movement and generally remain committed to activity in their own communities. The socialist-feminist movement has been unable to confront this phenomenon either theoretically or practically.

Toward a Unitary Theory of Women's Oppression

A review of the theoretical work produced in the context of the socialist-feminist movement reveals many significant themes. Taken together, they indicate the important contribution made by socialist feminism to the development of theory on the question of women.

Socialist-feminist theory starts from an insistence that beneath the serious social, psychological and ideological phenomena of women's oppression lies a material root. It points out that Marxism has never adequately analyzed the nature and location of that root. And it hypothesizes that the family constitutes a major if not the major terrain that nourishes it. With this position, socialist feminism implicitly rejects two currents in the legacy of socialist theory and practice on the question of women. First, the socialist-feminist emphasis on the material root of oppression counters an idealist tendency within the left, which trivializes the issue of women's oppression as a mere matter of lack of rights and ideological chauvinism. Second, socialist feminists' special concern with psychological and ideological issues, especially those arising within the family, stands opposed to an economic determinist interpretation of women's position, also common within the socialist movement. These perspectives establish guidelines for the socialist-feminist consideration of women's oppression and women's liberation.

Socialist feminists recognize the inadequacies as well as the contributions of Engels's discussion of the family and property relations in *The Origin of the Family, Private Property and the State.* Like

63

Engels, they locate the oppression of women within the dynamics of social development, but they seek to establish a more dialectical phenomenon as its basis than Engels was able to identify. Such a phenomenon must satisfy several implicit criteria. It must be a material process that is specific to a particular mode of production. Its identification should nevertheless suggest why women are oppressed in all class societies – or, for some in all known societies. Most important, it must offer a better understanding of women's oppression in subordinate as well as ruling classes than does Engels's critique of property. Socialist-feminist analyses share the view that childbearing, child-rearing and housework fit these criteria, although they offer a wide variety of theoretical interpretations of the relationship between these activities and women's oppression.

Some socialist feminists try to situate domestic labor within broader concepts covering the processes of maintenance and reproduction of labor power. They suggest that these processes have a material character and that they can be analyzed in terms of social reproduction as a whole. For elaboration of this position, which shifts the immediate theoretical focus away from women's oppression per se and onto wider social phenomena, they turn to Marx's writings, and especially to *Capital*. At the same time, they resist, as best they can, the contradictory pulls of economic determinism and idealism inherited from the socialist tradition.

The relationship between the capitalist wage and the household it supports represents yet another major theme. Socialist feminists point out that Marxism has never been clear on the question of whom the wage covers. The concept of the historical subsistence level of wages refers at times to individuals, and at other times to the worker 'and his family'. Recognition of this ambiguity has inspired a series of attempts to reformulate and answer questions concerning divisions of labor according to sex in both the family and wage labor. While some such efforts stress concepts of authority and patriarchy, others focus on questions involving the determination of wage levels, competition in the labor market and the structure of the industrial reserve army. Whatever the approach, the identification of the problem in itself constitutes a significant theoretical step forward.

Socialist-feminist theory also emphasizes that women in capitalist society have a double relation to wage labor, as both paid and unpaid workers. It generally regards women's activity as consumers and unpaid domestic laborers as the dominant factor shaping every woman's consciousness, whether or not she participates in wage labor. An important strategic orientation accompanies this view. Socialist feminists maintain, against some opinions on the left, that women can be successfully organized, and they emphasize the need for organizations that include women from all sectors of society. In support of their position, they point to the long history of militant activity by women in the labor movement, in communities and in social revolution. They observe, moreover, that mobilization demands a special sensitivity to women's experience as women, and they assert the legitimacy and importance of organizations composed of women only. It is precisely the specific character of women's situation that requires their separate organization. Here socialist feminists frequently find themselves in opposition to much of the tradition of socialist theory and practice. Socialist-feminist theory takes on the essential task of developing a framework that can guide the process of organizing women from different classes and sectors into an autonomous women's movement.

The strengths, richness and real contributions of socialist feminist theoretical work have made it more difficult to view Marxism as a rigid body of dogma brutally overwhelming the vital force of feminism in an unhappy marriage. Nonetheless, socialist feminist theory has been constrained by its practitioners' insufficient grasp of Marxism. With their roots in a practical commitment to women's liberation and to the development of a broad based autonomous women's movement, socialist feminists have only recently begun to explore their relationship to trends and controversies within the left. At the theoretical level, the exploration has taken the form of several waves of publications seeking, on the one hand, to delineate the substance of socialist feminism more clearly; and, on the other, to situate women's oppression more precisely within, rather than alongside, a Marxist theory of social reproduction.[29] In other words, the trial separation of Marxism and feminism is gradually coming to an end – not in a marriage, happy or unhappy, or in a divorce, but in the transcendence of contradictions that have festered between them for more than a century.

5 ENGELS'S *ORIGIN*: A DEFECTIVE FORMULATION

In the early 1970s, women's liberationists seeking an explanation of women's subordination often looked to traditional Marxist categories for inspiration. Many suggested that women and the family could be analyzed in terms of a human reproduction process comparable to but separate from commodity production. Support for this concept of a mode of reproduction could be found, they discovered, in Friedrich Engels's The Origin of the Family, Private Property and the State. *Their attempt to make women visible within social theory thus seemed to be endorsed by a founding father of radicalism.*

In this chapter, I offer a more careful reading of the text upon which women's liberationists relied for validation of their notions of a mode of reproduction. Engels's Origin *turns out to be a hastily assembled and contradictory work. To the extent that both the socialist tradition and contemporary feminism have relied on it for insight, their efforts to theorize women's oppression have been, I argue, confounded by its ambiguities.*

The Origin of the Family, Private Property and the State, by Friedrich Engels, has functioned as an authoritative text for both the socialist and the socialist feminist movements. In the socialist tradition, the text was the definitive Marxist pronouncement on the family and women's subordination. For socialist feminists in the 1970s, *Origin* likewise constituted a fundamental source. Generally wary of the Marxist tradition, these feminists nevertheless linked their theorizing to a passage from *Origin's* preface. What drew them was the assertion that social reproduction is fundamentally 'of a twofold character: on the one side, the production of the means of existence ...; on the other side, the production of human beings themselves'.[1] Through the repeated citation of this passage, Engels became the conveyor of official Marxist approval for the dualism of most socialist feminist theory.

This essay suggests that both the socialist tradition and today's socialist feminists have erred in their evaluation of *Origin*. Despite the book's significant contributions, it provides at most an unsteady point of departure for a theory of women's liberation.

Engels wrote *Origin* between March and May 1884, one year after Marx's death. The circumstances of his startlingly rapid production of the book remain mysterious. Writing to the German socialist Karl Kautsky on 16 February 1884, Engels described Marx's enthusiasm for the anthropological writings of the day, adding, 'if I had the time I would work up the material with Marx's notes, ... but I cannot even think of it'. Yet by late March he was already at work on *Origin* and by the end of April close to finishing it.[2] The full explanation of the reasons for Engels's change of plan, which is especially striking in view of the fact that he was already immersed in the editing of Marx's unfinished volumes of *Capital*, must await further research. It seems likely that the context was political. In 1879, the German socialist leader August Bebel had published *Woman in the Past, Present and Future*, which appeared in a revised version late in 1883. Tremendously popular from the start, Bebel's *Woman* bore the influence of emerging tendencies toward reformism within the socialist movement. Engels's decision to write *Origin* surely reflected a recognition of the weaknesses in Bebel's work. The socialist movement's commitment to women's emancipation required a more adequate foundation. Understood as an implicit polemic within the movement, *Origin* represented Engels's attempt to provide one.[3]

In drafting *Origin*, Engels relied principally on two sources: Lewis H. Morgan's *Ancient Society*, published in 1877, and a pair of notebooks in which Marx had entered passages from various authors, including Morgan, concerning early human society.[4] Morgan's text is thus complexly filtered as it makes its way into *Origin* – first by Marx in his notebooks and then again by Engels as he rereads Morgan in the light of Marx's notes. To grasp the meaning of *Origin*, it is therefore necessary to examine the assumptions and weaknesses of *Ancient Society* as well as the way Marx excerpted Morgan's text.

In *Ancient Society*, Morgan sought to demonstrate the parallel evolution of four 'characteristics' of human society: inventions and discoveries, government, family and property. Ranging across a vast array of ethnographic data, the book is divided into sections corresponding to the four characteristics. In the first, Morgan sketches three stages in the evolution of human inventions and discoveries.

At the most primitive level of social organization, peoples in the stage of 'savagery' gather wild plants, fish and hunt. The second period, 'barbarism', is characterized by food production, first horticulture and later agriculture. Finally, in the period of 'civilization', societies use advanced agricultural methods and keep written records. Morgan divides such societies into two broad types, ancient and modern. With this sequence of stages, he rests human history on a materialist foundation, but one whose essence is technological, not social.

Morgan devotes nearly two-thirds of *Ancient Society* to the second characteristic, government, tracing the evolution of social organization from early kin-based governance to the state. The social organization of the most primitive peoples is based simply on broadly defined 'classes' of persons permitted to marry one another. As the circle of possible marriage partners narrows, the 'gens', or clan, develops. In a 'gentile' society, an individual belongs to the clan of either mother or father, not to both. Living in northern New York state, Morgan believed he had observed the most developed form of gentile organization among the matrilineal Iroquois, a confederacy of tribes that included thousands of members governed through personal ties rather than formal political institutions. Eventually, clan organization gives way, pressed by technological advances in productivity. Property attains a dominant role and government can no longer rest on personal relations. Morgan sketches the early evolution of the state, which organizes people, now distributed in property classes, on a territorial basis.

Even before the emergence of developed political organization, a critical change occurs within the clan system. At a certain point, matrilineal clan organization succumbs to the principle of patrilineality. The impetus is the development of property. According to Morgan, descent through the female line is the original form of clan organization. As soon as property in cattle and land arises, however, two facts, entirely self-evident in Morgan's view, doom matrilineality. First, men naturally become the owners of the property. Second, they develop a natural wish to transmit it to their own children. Hence accumulation of property has the consequence that in the middle stages of barbarism, the patrilineal clan becomes the basic unit of the gentile social system.

A discussion of the third characteristic of human society, the family, follows, making up roughly one-quarter of *Ancient Society*. Morgan describes the evolution of five family forms, differentiated by progressive restriction of permissible marriage partners. He conjectures the first two as types of group marriage, 'consanguine' and 'punaluan', implying an even earlier stage of promiscuous intercourse. The third form, the 'pairing' family, is associated with clan-based societies. Single pairs marry and live in communal kin-based households; the marriage bond may be dissolved at will. Lineage ties remain primary for each partner, for the clan is the basic social unit. Morgan notes the collective security the pairing family system provides to individuals, as well as its egalitarianism when compared with subsequent family forms.

The last two family forms reflect the influence of the development of property. The 'patriarchal' family organizes a group of persons – slave, servant, free – under a male head who exercises supreme authority. The 'monogamian' family consists of a single couple which, with its children, composes an independent household. Morgan conceptualizes both family types as institutions whose primary purpose is to hold property and transmit it to offspring. To ensure the children's paternity, strict fidelity is required of women. Paternal power is more or less absolute, and only death can break the marriage bond. The patriarchal and monogamian families are forms more appropriate for political society; they appear in the last stages of barbarism and continue into the period of civilization.

Morgan argues that the patriarchal and monogamian families represent a social advance, for they permit a heightened individuality of persons. At the same time, he recognizes that in practice such individuality was available only to men. Women as well as children were generally subordinated to the paternal power of the family head. By contrast, the pairing family of clan society provided women with a certain level of equality and power, particularly before the transition to patrilineal descent. As long as children remained in their mother's clan, the pairing family was embedded in the matrilineal clan household, and Morgan thinks it likely that the woman rather than the man functioned as the family's center. With the shift to descent in the male line, the pairing family became part of the patrilineal clan household and the woman was more isolated from her gentile kin. Because she was still a member of her own clan, she nevertheless retained a measure of independent social standing. The advent of paternal power in the patriarchal and monogamian families opened the way to a profound degradation of women's position. Here the cruel subordination of women and children belies Morgan's optimistic notions of evolutionary development.

Ancient Society closes with a brief consideration of the fourth characteristic, property. Morgan distinguishes three stages in the development of property, generally corresponding to the three major evolutionary periods. Among the most primitive peoples, those at the level of savagery, property scarcely exists. Lands are held in common, as is housing, and Morgan speculates that the germ of property lies in a developing right to inherit personal articles. Property in land, houses and livestock emerges in the stage of barbarism. The rules of inheritance at first conform to clan organization: property reverts to the clan of the deceased, not to his or her spouse. Eventually, individual ownership through the monogamian family prevails, with property inherited by the deceased owner's children. The period of civilization has arrived.

In conclusion, Morgan offers the observation that in his own time property has become an 'unmanageable power'. Society is heading toward destruction, the logical outcome of a social organization in which 'property is the end and aim'. Still, Morgan holds out hope for society's reconstruction on 'the next higher plane', where it will appear to be 'a revival, in a higher form, of the liberty, equality and fraternity' of ancient clan society.[5]

Ancient Society is a monumental work. In it, Morgan solves the puzzle of clan organization, describes the sequence of social institutions in evolutionary terms, and analyzes the basis for their development. Published in 1877, *Ancient Society* became the foundation for all subsequent research on the history of early human societies, despite its many factual and interpretive errors. These shortcomings, as well as Morgan's substantial contributions, have been much discussed.[6] Here the emphasis will be on Morgan's understanding of the mechanisms of social change.

Morgan presents his material in parallel form, as 'four classes of facts' moving in parallel from savagery through barbarism to civilization. Each line constitutes 'a natural as well as necessary sequence of progress', but the impetus for the forward motion is not identified. Moreover, the discussion of the evolution of the family presupposes a grasp of the development of clan organization and vice versa. The extremely repetitive organization of *Ancient Society* reveals its author's inability to establish a clear relationship between his four kinds of phenomena. A theory of social development nonetheless lies implicit in Morgan's work. Frequently observing that 'the experience of mankind has run in nearly uniform channels', Morgan proposes that the placement of the major markers in these channels is determined by the evolution of the arts of subsistence – that is, by the types of inventions and discoveries used to acquire or produce the means of subsistence. In short, human progress ultimately rests on technological advances in the mode of material life.[7]

Morgan acknowledges the critical role played by property. The need to transmit property to heirs underlies, in his view, the shift from matrilineal to patrilineal clan organization. The rise of new 'complicated wants', growing out of an accelerated accumulation of property, brings about the dissolution of clan organization and its replacement by political society. But the nature of property remains relatively unexamined. For Morgan, property consists simply of things, the objects of subsistence, with no particular location within a network of social relations. Once the idea of property appears, it grows automatically, extending itself in both magnitude and complexity while nurturing a sequence of stages in the arts of subsistence. 'Commencing at zero in savagery, the passion for the possession of property, as the representative of accumulated subsistence, has now become dominant over the human mind in civilized races'. That is, a passion in the minds of men – greed – leads naturally to the evolution of property and, consequently, to technological advances and social development in general. [8]

Ancient Society captured the attention of many, among them Marx. In the 'Ethnological Notebooks', only published in the twentieth century, Marx included copious extracts from Morgan's book. Perhaps the most interesting feature of these notes is the way Marx revised the structure of *Ancient Society*, altering both the sequence of presentation and the relative weight of the sections. [9] Morgan had begun with the evolution of the arts of subsistence and had then surveyed the parallel development of government, family and property. Marx moved Morgan's long section on government to the end and altered the relative amount of space given to each part. He reduced by half the already short discussion of the arts of subsistence and by a third the section on the family. At the same time he extended, proportionately, the space given by Morgan to the consideration of property and government. In sum, Marx's notes rearrange Morgan's material as follows: arts of subsistence (reduced); family (reduced); property (expanded); government (slightly expanded). Through this reorganization Marx perhaps sought to put Morgan's findings into a theoretically more coherent order.

To the extent that Engels incorporated the material in *Ancient Society* into his *The Origin of the Family, Private Property and the State*, he adopted the order of Marx's excerpts in the 'Ethnological Notebooks' – making, however, several important structural changes. He did not devote a separate chapter to the subject of property. He greatly enlarged the relative importance of the chapter on the family, giving it almost as much space as he assigned to the chapters on the state. And he shifted the focus to the transition between barbarism and civilization. In this way, Engels converted Morgan's four 'lines of human progress' into three sections, which make up the bulk of *Origin*.

Substantively, Engels followed Morgan quite closely. He pruned the wealth of ethnographic evidence, even replacing it where his own studies offered more relevant data. He emphasized the points that most tellingly exposed the revised theoretical foundation he was seeking to establish. And he employed a more readable, even engagingly chatty, literary style. In general, *Origin* seems to be a shorter, more focused and more accessible version of *Ancient Society*. A closer examination of the ways in which Engels's presentation of the material differs from Morgan's reveals both the contribution and the limitations of *Origin*.

In a short opening Chapter 1, 'Stages in Prehistoric Culture', Engels succinctly recapitulates Morgan's account of the evolution of three stages in the arts of subsistence. Emphasizing the richness of Morgan's material, Engels also acknowledges a certain weakness in his own discussion, for not until the last chapter will he recast Morgan's work in the light of Marx's theory of social development. 'My sketch [is] flat and feeble compared with the picture to be unrolled at the end of our travels.' [10] As it turns out, *Origin* remains far closer to *Ancient Society* than Engels intended.

Chapter 2, 'The Family', constituting about one-third of *Origin*, presents a reworked and augmented version of Morgan's sequence of family types. Engels underscores the importance of Morgan's discoveries and takes the opportunity to situate the latter's work in the context of eighteenth- and nineteenth-century speculations concerning primate evolution, early human social behavior and the possibility of a primitive state of promiscuous sexual intercourse. Concluding these half-dozen pages with the observation that bourgeois moral standards cannot be used to interpret primitive societies, he comments on Morgan's discussion of the two hypothetical forms of group marriage. [11] Like Morgan, he believes that natural selection, through the innate mechanisms of jealousy and incest taboos, triggered the succession of family types. In addition, the logic behind the change Marx had made in Morgan's sequence of presentation now becomes clear, for Engels is able to explain the origin of the clan system in the course of his description of the punaluan family.

Having disposed of group marriage and the genesis of the clan, Engels turns to the pairing and patriarchal families. Here he merges the material Morgan had covered in his chapter on property into his discussion. Along with Morgan, Bachofen and others, Engels assumes that the supremacy of women characterized early human societies, but he argues that it rested on the material foundation of a natural sex division of labor within the primitive communistic household. Only if 'new, social forces' caused that natural material foundation to take a different form could women lose their position

of independence.[12] And this occurred when society began to produce a sizable surplus, making it possible for wealth to amass and
eventually pass into the private possession of families. Like Morgan,
Engels sees the development of productivity as an automatically
evolving process, but he makes a distinction, however vaguely,
between wealth as a given accumulation of things and private property as a social relation.

Once wealth is held privately, its accumulation becomes a central
social issue. 'Mother right' – descent in the female line and, along
with it, the supremacy of women in the communal household – now
constitutes a barrier to social development. Earlier, the supposedly
natural division of labor between women and men placed women in
charge of the household while men had the task of providing food.
In a society at a low level of productivity, therefore, women pos-
sessed the household goods and men the instruments necessary to
hunt, fish, cultivate plants and the like. With increasing productivity
and the development of private property in land, cattle and slaves,
this historical accident, as it were, has the grim consequence that
men, the former possessors of the instruments of gathering and
producing food, now own the wealth. Mother right makes it impossible, however, for men to transmit the newly evolved private property to their children. 'Mother right, therefore, had to be overthrown, and overthrown it was'.[13]

Engels regards the shift to the patrilineal clan system as pivotal
in its impact on society and on women's position. It marks the
establishment of a set of social relations conducive to the further
evolution not only of private property but of full-scale class
society. More dramatically:

> The overthrow of mother right was the *world historic defeat of
> the female sex*. The man took command in the home also; the
> woman was degraded and reduced to servitude; she became the
> slave of his lust and a mere instrument for the production of
> children.[14]

The patriarchal family, with its incorporation of slaves and serv-
ants under the supreme authority of the male head, now emerges
as a form intermediate between the pairing family and monogamy.
Engels offers specific historical examples of this transition stage,
emphasizing the relationship between land tenure and social
structure, as well as the brutality of the patriarch toward women
in the household.

In discussing the monogamous family, Engels again follows
Morgan while simultaneously incorporating a clearer analysis of

73

property relations and focusing on the question of woman's position. The monogamous family appears toward the end of the
second stage in the development of the arts of subsistence – that
is, at the threshold of civilization – and represents a perfected
form for the transmission of private property from father to children. Engels emphasizes the origin of the monogamous family in
economic conditions and its function as a property-holding institution. 'It was the first form of the family to be based not on
natural but on economic conditions – on the victory of private
property over primitive, natural communal property'.[15] Although
Engels never states it unambiguously, the implication is that the
form of the monogamous, as well as the patriarchal, family constitutes a product of the rise of class society.

Engels has no illusions about the position of women in the
monogamous family. Monogamy is a standard enforced on the
woman only, and exists solely to guarantee the paternity of the
offspring, not for any reasons of love or affection. Men are free
to live by a different standard. At the same time, the phenomenon of the neglected wife begets its own consequences. Thus
side by side with the institution of so-called monogamous marriage flourishes all manner of adultery and prostitution. Furthermore, 'monogamous marriage comes on the scene as the subjuga-
tion of the one sex by the other; it announces a struggle between
the sexes unknown throughout the whole previous prehistoric
period'. In Engels's formulation, this struggle between the sexes
appears simultaneously with class relations. 'The first class opposition that appears in history coincides with the development of the
antagonism between man and woman in monogamous marriage,
and the first class oppression coincides with that of the female
sex by the male'. Contrary to a common misinterpretation of
these remarks, Engels does not assert that the sex struggle pre-
dates class conflict. Neither, however, does he clearly argue that
it is rooted in the emergence of class society. He simply treats
the two developments as parallel, skirting the difficult problems of
historical origins and theoretical relationships.[16]

With the basic character of monogamous marriage established,
Engels turns briefly to a number of topics not addressed by Morgan. To begin, he presents a quick history of the monogamous
family's development in the period of civilization, with emphasis
on the extent to which it fostered 'individual sex love'. According
to Engels, love-based marriages were impossible prior to the great
'moral advance' constituted by the monogamous family. Moreover,
in all ruling classes, even after the rise of the monogamous family,
expedience rather than love governed the choice of marriage part-

ner. After a brief glance at the medieval ruling-class family, Engels focuses on marriage in capitalist society. Among the bourgeoisie, marriage is a matter of convenience, generally arranged by parents to further their property interests. By contrast, the proletariat has the opportunity truly to experience individual sex love. Among the proletariat:

> all the foundations of typical monogamy are cleared away. Here there is no property, for the preservation and inheritance of which monogamy and male supremacy were established; hence there is no incentive to make this male supremacy effective .... Here quite other personal and social conditions decide.

Moreover, Engels believes that with the increasing employment of women in wage labor, and women's accompanying independence, no basis survives for any kind of male supremacy in the working-class household, 'except, perhaps, for something of the brutality toward women that has spread since the introduction of monogamy'.[17]

Most of Engels's discussion of women's situation in capitalist society is framed in terms of the gap between formal and substantive equality.[18] He begins with an analogy between the marriage contract and the labor contract. Both are freely entered into, juridically speaking, thereby making the partners equal on paper. This formal equality disguises, in the case of the labor contract, the differences in class position between the worker and the employer. The marriage contract involves a similar mystification, since, in the case of a propertied family, parents actually determine the choice of children's marriage partners. In fact, the legal equality of the partners in a marriage is in sharp contrast with their actual inequality. Once the patriarchal and monogamous families develop, the wife's labor within the household becomes a private service. As Engels puts it, 'the wife became the head servant, excluded from all participation in social production'. Her work loses the public or socially necessary place it had held in earlier societies. Both excluded and, later, economically dependent, she therefore becomes subordinate. Only with large-scale capitalist industry, and only for the proletarian woman, does the possibility of reentry into production appear. Yet this opportunity has a contradictory character as long as capitalist relations endure. If the proletarian wife 'carries out her duties in the private service of her family, she remains excluded from public production and unable to earn; and if she wants to take part in public production and earn independently, she cannot carry out family duties'.[19]

Engels's conclusions regarding the conditions for ending women's subordination, summarized in a few paragraphs, generally converge with the equally brief remarks on the subject made by Marx in *Capital*. Like Marx, Engels underscores the progressive role that participation in the collective labor process can potentially play, and its crucial importance as a condition for human liberation. Where Marx had embedded his comments in an analysis of the historical impact of capitalist large-scale industry, Engels places his observations in the context of a discussion of political rights. He again draws an analogy between workers and women, arguing that both groups must have legal equality if they are to understand the character of their respective fights for 'real social equality'.

> The democratic republic does not do away with the opposition of [the proletariat and the capitalist class]; on the contrary, it provides the clear field on which the fight can be fought out. And in the same way, the peculiar character of the supremacy of the husband over the wife in the modern family, the necessity of creating real social equality between them and the way to do it, will only be seen in the clear light of day when both possess legally complete equality of rights.[20]

The discussion of women's oppression in Engels's chapter on the family marks a significant advance over *Ancient Society*. From the perspective of late twentieth-century socialist feminism, however, the account is problematic in many ways. Engels does not delineate the relationship between women's position and the emergence of class society. With respect to precapitalist class societies, he fails to specify the nature of women's subordination in different classes. For capitalism, he misses the significance of the working-class household as an essential social unit, not for the holding of property but for the reproduction of the working class itself. Thus he cannot see that a material basis for male supremacy is constituted within the proletarian household. Throughout the text he assumes that it is natural for 'family duties' to be the exclusive province of women. And he underestimates the variety of ideological and psychological factors that provide a continuing foundation for male supremacy in the working-class family. Finally, Engels's emphasis on the strategic importance of democratic rights leaves open the question of the relationship between socialist revolution, women's liberation and the struggle for equal rights. The result is ambiguous, potentially suggesting that the socialist program for women's liberation consists of two discrete objectives: equal rights with men in the still-capitalist short term; and full liberation on the basis of a higher form of the family in the far-distant revolutionary millennium.

Engels closes the chapter on the family with a long look to the future.[21] These pages attempt a sketch of family experience in a society in which the means of production have been converted into social property. True monogamy – that is, monogamy for the man as well as the woman – will now be possible, along with wide development of that highest of intimate emotions, individual sex love. Exactly what relations between the sexes will look like cannot be predicted, for this is up to a new generation of women and men born and raised in socialist society. Engels's focus on the emotional and sexual content of interpersonal relations within the family household reflected a common view that they represented the essence of the so-called woman question. Only at one point in this section does he dwell on the implications of the future abolition of the family's economic functions, observing that with the means of production held in common, 'the single family ceases to be the economic unit of society. Private housekeeping is transformed into a social industry'. Moreover, 'the care and education of the children becomes a public affair'.[22] These brief hints of programmatic guidance do not differ, in substance, from nineteenth-century communitarian proposals. In short, Engels's chapter on the family in *Origin* remains an unintegrated mix of Morgan's dry materialism and a radical view of sexual liberation – seasoned with genuine insights into the nature of property and social relations, and liberally sprinkled with Engels's warmth and wit.

In Chapters 3–8 of *Origin*, corresponding to the section on government in *Ancient Society*, Engels examines the nature of clan society and traces the rise of the state. As in Chapter 2 on the family, he follows Morgan's general line of argument, while at the same time incorporating the material on property. In Engels's words, the changes 'in form' between the institutions of the gentile constitution and those of the state 'have been outlined by Morgan, but their economic content and cause must largely be added by myself'.[23] The resulting discussion suffers from problems similar to those already observed in Engels's account of the family. Moreover, it becomes more obvious in these chapters that Engels identifies private property and the market exchange of commodities as the pivotal social developments in history. Nowhere, however, does he clearly discuss these phenomena in terms of the social relations that constitute the mode of production in which they originate.

In these chapters, a critique of property takes the place of a critique of class relations. Property, not exploitation – the appropriation of the surplus labor of the producing class by another class – becomes the implicit object of class struggle. From the point of view of Marx's theory of social reproduction, however, both private property and commodity exchange only represent specific manifestations of particular types of class society. In such societies, a given set of relations of exploitation always dominates, constituting the basis for specific social relations and forms of private property, the market, the state and so forth. The difference between this formulation and that in *Origin* is not simply a matter of style or manner of exposition. Rather, it indicates that Engels's arguments generally remain within the theoretical framework of a utopian critique of property. Marx's comments about Proudhon would apply also to Engels: he should have analyzed

> *property relations* as a whole, not in their *legal* expression as *relations of volition* but in their real form, that is, as *relations of production*. [Instead,] he has entangled the whole of these economic relations in the general juristic conception of *property*.

Furthermore, Engels has confused the circumstance that the products of labor are exchanged in a society, with the presence of capitalist, or at least class, relations of production.[24]

In *Origin*'s closing Chapter 9, 'Barbarism and Civilization', Engels examines the 'general economic conditions' behind the developments presented in previous chapters. He restates his account of social evolution in the period of the decline of clan society and the emergence of civilization, this time pointing out a series of major milestones. In the middle stages of barbarism, the separation of pastoral tribes from the mass of other peoples marks the 'first great social division of labor'. These tribes tame animals and develop agriculture; as a result they soon find themselves with products that make regular exchange possible. Inevitably and automatically, the increasing exchange leads to higher productivity, more wealth and a society in which the harnessing of surplus labor becomes feasible. Hence slavery appears. 'From the first great social division of labor arose the first great cleavage of society into two classes: masters and slaves, exploiters and exploited'. Engels reminds the reader that the change in the division of labor also has consequences for relations between the sexes in the family. Because the preexisting division of labor had supposedly assigned the task of procuring subsistence to men, men become the holders of the new wealth, and women find themselves subordinated and confined to private domestic labor. A 'second great division of labor' occurs at the close of the period

78

of barbarism, when handicraft separates from agriculture. On this basis, a new cleavage of society into classes develops, the opposition between rich and poor. Inequalities of property between individual male heads of families now lead to the break-up of the communal household, and the pairing marriage dissolves into the monogamous single family, even more oppressive to women. Finally, a third division of labor emerges in the period of civilization: a class of merchants arises, parasites whose nefarious activities lead to periodic trade crises. In the meantime, the rise of class cleavages has necessitated replacement of the gentile constitution with a third force, powerful but apparently above the class struggle – namely, the state.[25]

In sum, the concluding chapter of *Origin* argues that civilization results from the continual evolution of the division of labor, which in turn gives rise to exchange, commodity production, class cleavages, the subordination of women, the single family as the economic unit of society, and the state. What is problematic in this picture is that Engels once again simply lists phenomena without locating them in social relations and the workings of a dominant mode of production. Moreover, he awards the leading role to the technical division of labor in the labor process – what Morgan had considered under the rubric 'arts of subsistence'. The development of class cleavages simply follows automatically, once a certain level of material productivity is reached. In other words, the state of the forces of production mechanistically determines the nature of the relations of production. The emphasis on the technical division of labor in this chapter constitutes a new element, tending somewhat to replace the focus in earlier chapters on the rise of private property as the prime mover of social change. At the same time, Engels, like Morgan, often invokes innate human greed and competitiveness to explain historical development.[26] All in all, the scattered analysis of social development presented in this final chapter represents some of the least coherent reasoning in *Origin*.

Not surprisingly, Engels's concluding comments on the emancipation of women exhibit similar ambiguities. He emphasizes, yet again, the crushing impact of the 'first great social division of labor' on women's position, and then leaps to the supposedly self-evident conclusion that the entry of women into social production is emancipatory. As in the chapter on the family, Engels assumes that domestic labor is purely women's work, does not locate his statements about women with respect to a specific class society, and blurs the relationship between women's eventual liberation in communist society and immediate strategic goals.

Engels employed one argument in *Origin* that the socialist

movement later refused to endorse, but which has recently been taken up by theorists of the contemporary women's liberation movement. In a frequently cited passage from the preface, Engels speaks of two types of production proceeding in parallel:

> The determining factor in history is, in the final instance, the production and reproduction of immediate life. This, again, is of a twofold character: on the one side, the production of the means of existence, of food, clothing and shelter and the tools necessary for that production; on the other side, the production of human beings themselves, the propagation of the species. The social organization under which the people of a particular historical epoch and a particular country live is determined by both kinds of production: by the stage of development of labor on the one hand and of the family on the other. [27]

For socialist feminists, the citation of these sentences in article after article accomplishes several purposes. It affirms the socialist feminist commitment to the Marxist tradition. It suggests that Marx and Engels had more to say about the question of women than the later socialist movement was able to hear. It seems to situate the problem of women's oppression in the context of a theory of general social reproduction. It emphasizes the material essence of the social processes for which women hold major responsibility. And it implies that the production of human beings constitutes a process that has not only an autonomous character, but a theoretical weight equal to that of the production of the means of existence.

In short, this much-cited passage from *Origin*'s preface appears to offer authoritative Marxist backing for the socialist feminist movement's focus on the family, sex divisions of labor and unpaid domestic work, as well as for its theoretical dualism and its strategic commitment to the autonomous organization of women. Yet the passage actually reflects Engels at a theoretical weak point, perilously returning to an old unpublished manuscript written with Marx, the 'German Ideology'.

The dependence of *Origin* on the 'German Ideology' of 1846 is obvious, although rarely noted. Engels drew quite heavily on the forgotten manuscript of his and Marx's youth, which he had just rediscovered among Marx's papers. [28] In the passage from the preface, for example, the paralleling of the production of means of subsistence with the production of human beings recalls the earlier manuscript's discussion of the dual essence of social reproduction: 'The production of life, both of one's own in labor and of fresh life in procreation, ... appears as a twofold relation: on the one hand as a natural, on the other as a social relation'.[29] More generally, both texts make a sharp distinction between natural and social phenomena, emphasizing the purely biological or animal-like character of procreation. Furthermore, the 'German Ideology' assigns, as does *Origin*, a central motivating role in social development to the continual evolution of the division of labor. According to the 'German Ideology', society develops in stages, beginning with the simplest forms, in which the only division of labor is natural and is rooted in the sexual act. With the growth of the division of labor, social relations distinguish themselves from natural ones, and the 'family relation' becomes subordinate. Both the 'German Ideology' and *Origin* refer to the development, at this point in history, of a relationship of latent slavery within the family, representing 'the first form of property'.[30] Finally, both texts put forward an equivocal image of the family as a germ or nucleus within which larger social contradictions originate or are reflected, and which itself constitutes the fundamental building block of society.[31]

Engels's reliance on the 'German Ideology' has the effect of importing into *Origin* many of the weaknesses of the earlier manuscript. In particular, the positing of two separate systems of production of material life suggests a very primitive distinction between natural and social phenomena. Socialists at the turn of the century found the assertion concerning the duality of social reproduction 'very remarkable', indeed 'almost incomprehensible'. Soviet commentators eventually settled on the view that Engels was mistaken, and that the statement can only refer to the very earliest period of human history, when people were supposedly so much a part of nature that social relations of production could not be said to exist.[32] What disturbed these theorists was the implication that the family represents an autonomous, if not wholly independent, center of social development. And it is precisely this implication that has caught the imagination of contemporary socialist feminists.

Engels's purpose in writing *Origin* was 'to present the results of Morgan's researches in the light of the conclusions of [Marx's] materialist examination of history, and thus to make clear their full significance'.[33] Engels's treatment of the material falls short of this goal, however, for he only partially transforms Morgan's crude materialism. *Origin* is marred throughout by Engels's failure to base the discussion on an adequate exposition of Marx's theory of social development. Instead, Engels relies, quite erratically, on several theoretical frameworks in addition to his understanding of Marx's work: the technological determinism implicit in Morgan's *Ancient Society*, his main source of data; the 'German Ideology's' early version of historical materialism; and a generally utopian critique of property and view of the socialist future. While *Origin* manages, in places, to rise above this eclecticism, its theoretical incoherence was to have serious consequences. *Origin* constitutes a defective text whose ambiguous theoretical and political formulations nevertheless became an integral part of the socialist – and, more recently, the socialist feminist – undertaking.

6 FROM THE WOMAN QUESTION TO WOMEN'S LIBERATION

How can Marxist theory address the problem of women's oppression? For most of the 1970s I wrestled with this conundrum. Beyond a critique, I wanted to come up with an alternative. First in 'Questions on the Woman Question' (Chapter 2 of this book) and then more fully in Marxism and the Oppression of Women: Toward a Unitary Theory, *published in 1983, I offered the beginnings of a materialist analysis that put childbearing and the oppression of women at the heart of every class mode of production.*

Central to my approach was a confrontation with the Marxist tradition on the woman question. Texts long regarded by socialists as canonical in fact offered, I thought, only an unstable hodgepodge of fragments pertaining to women. I therefore undertook a lengthy critical reading of such concepts as the reproduction of labor power, individual consumption, and the industrial reserve army as they appeared in the writings of Marx, Engels, Bebel, Lenin, Zetkin and others. Once disentangled, reworked and supplemented, these concepts became the starting point for the construction of a more adequate theoretical framework.

This chapter provides an overview of what that framework might look like. Responding to a 1983 critique by Johanna Brenner and Nancy Holmstrom, I challenge conventional socialist feminist analysis of women's oppression in capitalist societies on two counts.[1] Where socialist feminists commonly locate women outside the processes of capitalist accumulation, I position them at their center. And where socialist feminists often assume female subordination to be rooted solely in women's relation to the economy, I argue that it is established by their dual situation, differentiated by class, with respect to domestic labor and equal rights. That is, capitalism stamps the sub-

83

ordination of women with a twofold character, political as well as economic.

My advocacy of Marxist-feminist theory did not come at an auspicious moment. In the early 1980s neither of my intended audiences was likely to pay much attention. The US left, never that strong and always hostile to feminism's supposedly inherent bourgeois tendencies, was losing ground in an increasingly conservative political climate. American feminism, by contrast, had at last achieved a more mainstream, if always vulnerable, acceptance, together with new kinds of concerns. Several years after the unhappy marriage of Marxism and feminism seemed to have ended in divorce (see Chapter 4 above), socialist feminism was a minor trend within the rapidly growing women's movement.

Meanwhile, postmodernist theorists had launched a quite persuasive attack on the Enlightenment notion of a universal human subject – autonomous, coherent, unencumbered, and without gender, race or class. In many ways a theorization of understandings developed by the social movements of the 1960s, this analysis also entailed rejection of the modernist quest for an all-embracing single theory. Postmodernists targeted Marxism as an emancipatory grand narrative that had to be abandoned. To argue in 1983 for a unitary Marxist-feminist theory was thus to be, at the very least, seriously out of step.

Readers will notice that I take issue with the claim that empirical accounts of the history of women constitute the appropriate basis for feminist theory. This is because I resist the temptation to collapse theory into history or, more generally, to theorize directly 'from experience'. Theory, it seems to me, is necessarily abstract and quite limited in its role. I find it helpful to use a metaphor. Theory is something like a skeleton – different from but necessary to the flesh and blood data of history it supports. A skeleton must be structurally coherent, of course, but the Marxist theoretical tradition fails to meet this condition. In my work I therefore put a great deal of effort into the rigorous reconstruction of a set of concepts pertinent to women's position within social reproduction. When, for example, I define domestic labor or generational replacement and consider their articulation within the social reproduction of class-stratified societies, I only identify possible mechanisms and tendencies. These can then be of use in the study of a specific historical situation, but the scope of what they can explain is severely restricted. Even less can they directly suggest strategy or an evaluation of the prospects for political action. These are matters for concrete analysis and historical investigation. The bare bones of theory only spring to life, in other words, when they encounter the rich data of history.[2]

In 'Questions on the Woman Question' (*Monthly Review*, June 1979; Chapter 2 in the present volume), I addressed the problem of the relationship between women's liberation and the struggle for socialism in three ways. First, I criticized the ambiguities of theoretical work in the socialist tradition on the so-called woman question. Second, I sketched what I believe to be a more rigorous theoretical approach. Third, I offered a brief consideration of strategic orientations. Packing so much into the article format, I was unavoidably too brief and some of what I wrote is open to misinterpretation. I am therefore happy to have this opportunity to respond to Johanna Brenner and Nancy Holmstrom's comments and to clarify my analysis of women's oppression.

The bulk of 'Questions on the Woman Question' consisted of a critique of the socialist tradition. I organized my discussion in terms of an opposition between two approaches, then called the 'family argument' and the 'social production argument'. I now conceptualize these as the 'dual-systems perspective' and the 'social reproduction perspective', and I continue to believe that only the latter can adequately situate women's oppression within the framework of Marx's analysis of social development. This position has little in common, however, with the view attributed to me by Brenner and Holmstrom, namely that 'women's oppression stems from their marginalization from social production'. I seek to understand women's oppression in terms of the differential location of women and men *within*, not at the edge of, the social reproduction processes of class society, most especially those involving the reproduction of labor power.

To theorize women's oppression, I do not take the notions of reproduction of labor power and domestic labor for granted, as is common in the socialist feminist literature. For example, I restrict the meaning of reproduction of labor power to the processes that maintain and replace exploitable labor power. That is, the concept is pertinent only to subordinate classes. (Propertied-class women also experience gender oppression, but it is associated with their role in the maintenance and reproduction of the property-owning class, not of labor power.) I also detach the concept of reproduction of labor power from customary assumptions of biological procreation in family contexts. Although the reproduction of labor power usually involves child-rearing within kin-based settings called families, it can be organized in other ways. From a theoretical point of view, it does not necessarily entail heterosexuality, family forms, or even generational replacement. That these institutional arrangements are so common reflects their advantages over the alternatives.[3]

In capitalist societies, labor power takes the form of a commodity and the reproduction of labor power has specific features, shaped in the workings of capitalist social reproduction. At its heart is working-class women's historically evolved, disproportionate responsibility for domestic labor. By domestic labor I do not mean housework but, rather, a particular set of activities involving the maintenance and replacement of the bearers of labor power and of the working class as a whole. Capitalism stamps this domestic labor with its own character: as in no other mode of production, maintenance and replacement tasks become spatially, temporally and institutionally isolated from the sphere of production, with serious consequences for relations between working-class women and men and for the nature of women's oppression.

Domestic labor constitutes, I also suggest, an important but heretofore invisible component of what Marx termed necessary labor. As such it is both indispensable to capital and an obstacle to accumulation. If capitalist production is to take place, it must have labor power – the essential force that propels its advance. And if labor power is to be available, domestic labor must be performed. At the same time, domestic labor to some extent stands in the way of capitalism's drive for profit, for it limits the availability of labor power that might otherwise be exploited in the value-producing process. The capitalist class is thus caught between the conflicting pressures of its long-term need for a labor force, its short-term requirements for different categories of workers and its desire to maintain hegemony over a divided working class. In response it adopts a variety of strategies, some of which involve manipulating domestic labor in ways that create absolute or relative surplus value.[4]

Over the long term, the capitalist class seeks to stabilize the reproduction of labor power at a low cost and with a minimum of domestic labor. At the same time, the working class strives to win the best conditions for its own renewal, which may include a particular level and type of domestic labor. Because both capital and labor are ordinarily fragmented into distinct sectors, the results are not uniform across the working class. A contradictory tendential dynamic thus threads through historical struggles over the conditions for the reproduction of labor power. Particular outcomes include the family wage for certain groups, protective legislation covering female and child industrial workers, sex- and race-segregation in the labor market, migrant labor housed in barracks and so forth.

While only certain women perform domestic labor in capitalist society, all women suffer from lack of equality. Women's lack of

86

equality constitutes a specific feature of women's oppression in capitalist societies. As Marx and Lenin argued, equality of persons is not an abstract principle or false ideology but a complex tendency with roots in the articulation of the spheres of production and circulation. 'Capitalism', observed Lenin, following Marx, 'combines formal equality with economic and, consequentially, social inequality'.[5]

Given the contradictory character of equality in capitalist society, struggles to expand its scope threaten the dominance of capitalist social relations on two fronts. First, they tend to reduce divisions within and among oppressed classes, as well as between these classes and other sectors, by moving all persons toward a more equal footing. Second, they reveal the foundation of bourgeois society to be class exploitation, not individual equality, for the further democratic rights are extended, the more capitalism's oppressive economic and social character stands revealed. Far from a useless exercise in reformism, the battle for equality can point beyond capitalism.

Lack of equality as a group constitutes the basis for movements that bring women from different classes and sectors together – movements that Holmstrom, Brenner and I agree are critical to socialist transformation. These movements may hold varying interpretations, explicit or implicit, of the meaning of the equality they seek. Some, for example, may regard equality of women and men within capitalist society as a sufficient goal. The contradictions of modern capitalism make it likely, however, that twentieth-century women's movements will have at least some insight into the deficiencies of a liberal conception of equality. This can form a basis for the development of a women's movement oriented toward socialism, as recent historical research documents.[6] Since the 1960s, women's movements in the advanced capitalist countries as well as in some Third World countries have also shown such potential. Unfortunately, the left has rarely been capable of intervening constructively. Its weakness has its origin, in part, in the lack of an adequate theory of women's oppression and of the role of the demand for equality and democratic rights in social change.

To sum up my theoretical position: the logic of capitalist accumulation and the articulation between the spheres of production and circulation doubly constitute women's subordination. On the one hand, women and men are differentially located with respect to important material aspects of social reproduction. On the other, women, like other groups, lack full democratic rights. The dynamics of female oppression in capitalist society respond to this dual situation, varying along dimensions of social class, race, ethnicity, etc.

Women in capitalist societies, in short, have a distinctive political as well as economic location. Their disadvantaged position in the political sphere is a phenomenon that is analytically separable from, yet rooted in, their subordinate place within capitalist relations of production. Marxists who ignore this political aspect of women's status in capitalist societies open themselves up to the age-old canard that takes Marxism to be a theory of economic determinism.

In their critique, Brenner and Holmstrom misread my theorization of social reproduction and ignore my discussion of equal rights, thereby generally distorting the theoretical approach I propose. Along with much socialist and socialist feminist analysis, they argue that 'women's oppression is a function of both their role in the family and their role in wage labor'. That is, they locate female oppression in women's dual position as domestic workers and wage-laborers. The problem with this kind of analysis is that it focuses solely on economic phenomena, fails to account for the oppression of nonworking-class women, and cannot explain the basis for movements of women that cross class, race and other divisions. Despite professed commitments to the liberation of all women, to organizational autonomy and to the importance of subjective experience, activists who hold this view paradoxically embrace an analysis of women's oppression with weaknesses quite similar to those of the socialist tradition. By contrast, I consider women's oppression in terms of their dual position with respect to domestic labor and equal rights. In this way I offer a framework for both analyzing working-class women's position and understanding how a broad-based women's liberation movement may represent an essential component in the struggle for socialism.

In making their comments, Brenner and Holmstrom claim to offer 'a theory of women's oppression based on the actual conditions of material production'. In their view, theory is built out of full-blown historical accounts of the evolution of social relations. In contrast, I distinguish between history and theory and my presentation is necessarily abstract.[7] My critics' disappointment in the theoretical adequacy of my arguments thus reflects a misplaced demand for detailed empirical descriptions of the history of women's oppression. Historical accounts alone, no matter how detailed and accurate, cannot provide a theoretical foundation.

Where my emphasis in 'Questions on the Woman Question' was on theory, Brenner and Holmstrom focus on the practical questions facing socialist feminists and socialists committed to women's liberation. As a basis for their strategic outlook, they examine the evolution of women's oppression in the course of capitalist development. From this history they derive a strategic corollary: women must organize 'separate from and independent of men'. Such self-organization must include both a women's movement and women's caucuses in all mass organizations as well as socialist organizations. In contrast, I suggested that such questions were strictly a matter of concrete analysis and some readers have concluded that I do not support the independent organization of women. Let me restate my views ,more positively. Because of the history of women's oppression and the revolutionary edge inherent in the issue of democratic rights, it seems highly likely to me that the independent organization of women will be and must be a feature of struggles for socialism – both before and after the attainment of state power. I see this, however, as a strategic orientation flowing from concrete analysis rather than an abstract principle of socialist organization. Despite their disclaimer, Brenner and Holmstrom come dangerously close, I think, to the position that 'organizational structure provides an ironclad guarantee' of commitment to women's interests.

In conclusion, I want to observe that my critics and I agree on many points. Above all, we share what Gail Omvedt has delineated as a socialist feminist outlook – 'a feeling of a need for revolutionary change and a genuine commitment to the left, coupled with a distrust not only of the bourgeois establishment but also of the traditional left bureaucracy and its economistic neglect of women's oppression'. And we share as well the view that, as Crystal Eastman put it, 'we will not wait for the Social Revolution to bring us the freedom we should have won in the nineteenth century'.[8]

III Difference, Diversity and Equality

7 CLASS AND OTHER ROOTS

This essay, a response to an article by Karen Sacks published in Monthly Review, is the oldest I have included in this book. Written in 1976, its language and tone now seem quaint, reflecting the polemics of earlier times. But the concerns I voiced remain relevant.

My purpose in the article was to demonstrate the pertinence of feminist scholarship and theorizing to questions posed by the left. I pointed to recent historical research – the 'new' social history – for better ways to tell the story of women. I critiqued the tendency of labor historians and Marxist theorists to rely on an economic determinist analysis of social change. I called for a more rigorous (and, ideally, collective) effort to confront the so-called woman question as a theoretical problem.

I also questioned the then-common assumption that sex, class and race can be paralleled as co-equal phenomena. Such a methodology produced nonsensical results, I thought, and I documented instances of the theoretical incoherence, historical misinterpretation and political difficulties entailed. To theorize the relationship of race, class and gender on the model of mechanically interacting systems would not, in my view, get us very far. At the time, however, I was unable even to gesture in the direction of a more adequate approach.

The problem of finding alternative frameworks for theorizing diversity has become if anything more acute in the 1990s. The notion that race, class and gender are comparable systems meshed together in a complex mechanism remains popular, however. Race, class and gender continue to be described as interlocking, interactive, inextricably intertwined systems. The metaphors are telling. Despite much effort to develop more dynamically integrated conceptualizations, the model retains a stubbornly mechanical character. Multiple systems enter into ever more complicated interrelations, but each system itself remains unproblematically coherent and unified. Far more promising, I think, are recent attempts, particularly by feminists of color, to use postmodernist theory to examine the meanings of race, class and gender as inherently unstable and shifting.[1]

In recent years, historians and social theorists of all political persuasions have responded to the rapidly changing participation of women in various spheres of social life by taking up, once again, 'the woman question'. For the left the issue should be especially acute, for our goal is to transform the very conditions within which this so-called woman question has been posed. Such a transformation involves the development of theory, of concrete analyses of the current situation, and of strategy and practice.

Among our tasks, then, is the construction of a Marxist history of the entity that is our concern when we try to answer 'the woman question'. Karen Sacks's article in the February 1976 issue of *Monthly Review*, 'Class Roots of Feminism', is a serious attempt to contribute to this undertaking. Unfortunately, it reinforces certain traditional shortcomings within the left concerning 'the woman question'.

Sacks's main point is that one can best understand US women's activism between 1820 and 1920 (and, by implication, today as well) as consisting not of 'a single movement, but rather three movements which were consciously movements for the rights of women' – a working-class women's movement, a white middle-class women's movement and a Black women's movement. Working-class women fought for economic demands, white middle-class women for legal equality and Black women (class unknown) for 'both economic improvement and legal equality with whites'. Where the movements came into conflict, class (or sometimes race) antagonisms predominated over sex solidarity. Although victories were at times won, the contradictions persist. Today 'the two longstanding working-class women's demands' for equal pay and for unionization remain. Sacks considers the present situation to be promising, because 'middle-class women's jobs have become collectivized [and] middle-class women have also moved into union situations, which at least provide a material basis for middle-class women to join working-class women rather than the ruling class'.

Few on the left would disagree that the issue of class is at the root of this history. (Some maintain that there are two such roots – class and patriarchy. However, a coherent definition of patriarchy, together with a theory of its dual origin, has not yet been elaborated.) What is currently being debated is precisely how. Rather than participating in this debate as it is evolving, Sacks relies on a more orthodox array of concepts. Class is defined as the sole source of one's social outlook. Demands are then narrowly categorized and assigned according to class. (No mention is made of the analytical problems involved – what the terms working class and middle class mean as one moves through the decades from 1820 to 1920 and what they signify today.) Similarly, types of action are correlated with class situations: working-class women find themselves in collective on-the-job situations and take collective action, while middle-class women lean toward individualistic solutions. Finally, Sacks argues that each of her women's movements identifies the enemy differently, with only the working-class movement understanding that 'it [is] clearly the employer'.

Sacks's article reflects the economism that permeates much historical research carried out from a left perspective. Economism, understood in the most general sense, tries to reduce all social experience to economic phenomena. At the heart of these phenomena is the class struggle, conceived as a solely economic contradiction which manifests itself mainly in workplace situations. All else is in some sense secondary or superstructural, having at most a modifying effect on the more basic economic developments. The economic is thus separated from other realms of social experience by a clean line; the intuitive obviousness of this separation is not questioned.

In Sacks's article, economism plays a dominant role. Class is conceptualized as a plain mixture of 'material conditions' and externally imposed ideology. A mechanistic dynamic of economic forces is the cause of every social development. Sacks claims, for example, that the demands of the working-class movement throughout its history have been mostly economic and workplace-oriented, thus leaving political goals to middle-class movements. Moreover, she implies that when the working class organizes collectively in its fight against the enemy – identified as the employers, not the bourgeoisie as a class – it wins. The suggestion that the goals of the working class are actually attainable through militant struggle within capitalism is a direct consequence of economism. Such an approach to history does not seriously take into account struggles outside the workplace or issues of democratic rights, much less the question of the state and the problems of class consciousness and revolutionary organization. In other words, it ignores the real object of the class struggle: political power and social revolution.

Sacks's economistic assumptions influence her treatment of social movements. The article is organized around an initial assertion that there were three nineteenth-century women's movements based, respectively, on sex, class and race. The text then follows the three movements through time as each consciously fights for the

95

rights of women. But what was this activism in reality? The white middle-class movements[2] were made up mostly of women and tended to have as their primary goal the concerns of women; thus it is reasonable to call them conscious women's movements. By contrast, the working-class organizations discussed by Sacks were not in fact women's movements at all, nor were they consciously in favor of women's rights. They were trade unions, only rarely segregated according to sex (and then only at the local level) and never taking the rights of women workers *as women* as a primary objective. What Sacks is pointing to are certain moments when, for various reasons (ranging from opportunism to the sporadic recognition that the goal of sex equality can unify rather than divide the class), the working-class movement took up issues touching on women's rights. By the 'Black women's movement' Sacks seems to be referring to a range of antislavery organizations before the Civil War, to the situation of Black people after the war and to the rise of the middle-class Black women's club movement. As she herself acknowledges, Black activism crossed class lines; its major focus was slavery and, later, racism. Issues of class and sex were at times important, but the alleged existence of a Black women's movement which was consciously a movement for the rights of women is Sacks's weakest construction.

What is the basis of this attempt to delineate three parallel women's movements? It is the notion, common among left feminists, that first assumes sex, class and race oppression to be parallel, and then ranks them. For each oppression a movement arises. Qualitative (for example, political) differences between the movements are reduced to quantitative disparities that can be weighed and measured: the balance of forces is evaluated according to a uniform scale of strength (numbers of workers, length of strikes, level of militancy, etc.). In order to rank the three parallel oppressions and movements Sacks must then declare the priority of one of them: class. Class is simply the right answer to the unstated question of which of the three movements is to be considered the best or strongest in some value hierarchy of the left. In short, the claim that class is the key turns out to be simply a moral imperative, not a principle of analysis or social theory.

Contrary to Sacks's intentions, class functions as only one of three co-equal contradictions. The relationships between the contradictions are not explained. The fundamental role of the class struggle is in effect obscured. The real problems – in particular, those concerning the nature and status of sex, class and race issues in a society dominated by the capitalist mode of production – remain to be confronted.

Sacks's general approach is thus theoretically and politically flawed. Similar weaknesses appear in her treatment of the particulars of history, for her methodological assumptions lead her to ignore the results of more than a decade of 'new' social history. This work has attempted to correct some of the inadequacies of an older tradition of labor history. Rather than focusing narrowly on workers' organization, ideology and political activity, 'new' social historians seek to study the whole fabric of social life. The results of the new research in terms of empirical material have been extremely important. In particular, the history of working-class experience can now go beyond the overemphasis, characteristic of traditional labor history, on workers on the job and in their collective organizations and actions. Moreover, certain groups that were once virtually absent from historical accounts – women, for instance – have become more visible.

As an example of how the recent research in social history might have been used, consider Sacks's discussion of the women who worked in the early textile industry. In her account, the workers in the mills were at first young unmarried farm women who stayed in factory work for only short periods. But after the business crisis of 1837, mill workers 'were, by and large, landless native-born and Irish immigrants who could no longer quit if wages and hours were unsatisfactory'. The combination of oppressive working conditions and a collective workplace situation quite naturally gave rise to organization. Demands were purely economic and they were pursued solely through collective action. Although the movement was centered in New England, the biggest struggle somehow took place in western Pennsylvania, where militant workers struck in 1845 and again in 1848 for nearly two months. Some gains were won, and all in all 'these early textile battles show the militance and leadership women gave to the early labor movement'.

There are numerous inadequacies in this version of history. New England farm women temporarily sojourning in the mill towns still made up more than four-fifths of the workforce throughout the late 1840s; even in the 1850s about half the workers were Yankee women. Individual acts of resistance as well as spontaneous strikes were frequent from the 1820s onwards. Sustained collective action, carried out by a number of shortlived labor-reform associations and newspapers, spanned a period of six or seven years in the 1840s, and then came to an abrupt stop. The object of some of these actions went well beyond the purely economic, and indeed the borders between so-called economic and other types of goals were especially permeable in the nineteenth century. Most important, militancy, consciousness and organization were not, as Sacks suggests, the automatic or predetermined products of collective oppression. Nor was the response of these mostly Yankee women – the first American factory workers – monolithically the same. In order to reconstruct their experience and grasp its significance, one must do more than focus on organizational forms and militant struggles.

This is not the place to provide a better account of the New England mill women and their organizations. The textile workers constitute a very specific example in Sacks's article, and social historians may well challenge much of her other material and interpretations. Here, as elsewhere, the fundamental problem is her reliance on the economism of conventional labor history, which obscures the importance of considering nonworkplace issues and limits the scope of the class struggle.

In conclusion, I would like to sketch the outlines of an alternative approach to the problems discussed in this critique. What is at stake, I think, is the distinction between Marxism and revisionism – a line that I doubt has ever been clearly and broadly drawn for 'the woman question'. Indeed, I would argue that despite a century of work and in some cases the best of intentions, we do not even have an adequate knowledge of what the object of 'the woman question' is. The economism of Sacks's article and its reformist consequences are unfortunately not all that different from the Marxist tradition in this area. They are easy to criticize, but the process of building a serious alternative has just begun. In this context, Althusser's remark that the results of recent theoretical work can have '*revolutionary* effects in the fields which this science has not yet really touched' is useful.[3] Surely 'the woman question' is such a field.

What then is needed to understand the phenomena Sacks discusses and to start to unravel 'the woman question'? First, a great deal more empirical work must be done, for we are barely at the level of a descriptive understanding. This work should be informed by a consistent political outlook and avoid the traditional errors of economism: isolation of on-the-job from all other experience, overemphasis on economic issues, assumptions that working-class goals are restricted to the economic sphere. One approach would be to choose topics in order intentionally to cross the borders set up by economism. For example, recent work by social historians has focused on subjects on either side of those borders, such as family life in given groups, the development of specific residential communities, the trade union experience of certain women workers, the labor process in various industries, the history and meaning of scientific management. We must design studies – of contemporary as well as of historical situations – that force an integration of all relevant aspects and define their limits mainly in terms of space and time.

Empirical work can provide only some of the preconditions for an elaborated theory that will begin to resolve 'the woman question' in a rigorous manner. It is impossible to specify the substance of this theory in advance, but some observations may be made. The theory will have to go beyond description, partial analyses and pragmatic politics. It must confront 'the woman question' in terms of Marxist theory. This will probably mean, among other things, developing analyses along several dimensions: an understanding of the reproduction of labor power and of the process Marx called individual consumption; a critique of the family to the extent that it is an ideological concept; and a theory of the variant forms of family possible in societies dominated by the capitalist mode of production. In the past several years some useful work has been done on these questions, but the efforts have remained essentially isolated. [4] If future work can build on previous advances, including where necessary a certain amount of comradely polemicizing, we may soon replace the theoretical component of 'the woman question' with a more meaningful concept. Inasmuch as revolutionary politics is rooted in Marxist theory, we may also be closer to developing an analysis and strategy that can effectively be put into practice.

8 TELLING TALES: HISTORIANS OF OUR OWN LIVES

This article originated in my puzzlement as I prepared to be the discussant at a session of the Eighth Berkshire Conference on the History of Women, held in 1990 at Douglass College, New Brunswick, NJ. The papers on which I was to comment assumed a particular account of the evolution of women's history and feminist theory. Despite being involved in the developments that led to the new feminist scholarship, I did not recognize the tale they told.

The papers presented at my session were symptomatic of a broader trend. Something had happened to flatten the complicated history of second-wave feminism into a cautionary moral tale. Gone was the exhilarating complexity of the women's liberation movement, with its radical decentralization, its many debates over theoretical and political questions and its links to other social movements. Missing as well were the early contributions of women of color and working-class women, soon joined by lesbian women, disabled women, women from the range of marginalized sectors. Missing too, despite the printed record, were their voices – patiently and impatiently insisting (and never really being heard by most feminists) that a women's liberation movement worth its name had to include us all. In place of this productive polyphony came a simpler narrative that pinned feminism onto an evolutionary path. In the academic version of this story, feminist scholarship progressed steadily from the simplistic early efforts of well-meaning white middle-class PhDs to ever-greater methodological sophistication, substantive accomplishment and sensitivity to diversity.

I wanted to understand better what this revision of the history of second-wave feminism meant. Along with others who had participated in the movements of the 1960s, I especially resented the common assertion that issues of race and class were not of interest to feminists until the 1980s.[1] *In my remarks at the conference I was full of indignation at the distortion of the true history of women's history.*

It has since become clearer to me that the story I did not recognize is not so much false as hegemonic. One reason it has achieved this position of prominence is that it resonates well with popular understandings promulgated in the media. Another is that its chronicle of perpetual improvement seems to reflect lived experience – as constructed from the standpoint of white women whose feminist formation occurred after the mid-1970s in elite college and graduate school settings. For these women, the first meaningful encounter with issues of race often came in the form of a personal confrontation.[2] Where in the 1960s and early 1970s racism and white privilege were inescapable questions of public concern, by the 1980s it required the entry of scholars of color into the upper halls of academe to make many of their white colleagues take notice.

A surprising consensus supports this ideologically dominant account of the development of the modern women's movement and of feminist scholarship. It is surprising because it includes feminists of color as well as those who are white and because a number of today's feminist academics go back to the 1960s and early 1970s – when they perhaps marched, demonstrated and organized (or at least observed others doing so), even as they studied and wrote. What has happened, I wonder, to make us forget the salience of issues of race and class in those years? The consensus is all the more perplexing in the light of the popularity of postmodernist theory, which forcefully counsels a mistrust of unitary narratives.

The currency of the dominant story of course depends on the suppression of alternative versions, a process I believe occurred in the late 1970s and early 1980s.[3] In the 1990s the suppression is returning to haunt feminist scholarship as it strains to embrace diversity. The real trick, not easily achieved, is to make sense of the world as, in historian Elsa Barkley Brown's words, a 'gumbo ya ya ... everybody talking at once, multiple rhythms being played simultaneously'.[4] Given our classical training, it is easier for most of us to hear one melody at a time and to pay more attention to the stronger voices. But if we follow Barkley Brown's recommendation that we learn to listen and compose in a different way, we may discover a powerful new music of many songs, travelling and crossing over and doubling back.

Metaphors help us to speculate, to think beyond existing theories and models, to envision what we cannot yet specify.[5] Gumbo ya ya, multiple rhythms, polyphony, palimpsest – these figures appeal to me as pointing to a transcendence of the classical orchestration.[6] Perhaps new efforts to pay attention to the gumbo ya ya of multiple truths[7] – some securely proclaimed from center stage, others spoken or even *shouted from the wings but ignored – will more persuasively tell the story of feminist scholarship.*

The comments I make here flow from the experience I had reading and rereading two papers[8] in preparation for the 1990 Berkshire Conference on the History of Women. My perplexity centered on the way the authors, Louise Newman and Joan Williams, placed their analyses within the larger framework of the development of women's history and feminist theory over the previous two decades. Although I had been actively involved during the years in which the new women's history emerged, I did not recognize the story they told. In the remarks that follow, I examine the pieces of the story that baffled me, and I put the puzzle together another way.

A Straw Women's History

In the course of addressing the substantive issues in their papers, Newman and Williams touch very briefly on the origins and development of the field of women's history. They rely on a version of this academic subspecialty's history that is apparently commonplace; indeed, Newman and Williams present the facts as unproblematic. But the narrative they offer – which Newman and Williams have simply adopted, not invented, and for which they are therefore not really responsible[9] – has serious problems. In order to consider what these problems entail, I must first retell the story.

In the beginning, according to this widely believed account, there was women's history. These were the bad old days, when feminist historians had to stumble forward using what limited tools they could find or fashion. Despite their best efforts, these pioneers could not help but make errors. In particular, they made three. First, they viewed women as an undifferentiated group sharing an essential womanhood; that is, they ignored such factors as race, class, ethnicity, age and sexual orientation. Second, they relied upon a simplistic opposition of the domestic to the public sphere and sought to validate women's culture and the domestic sphere as sources of women's strength. Third, they utilized a pedestrian epistemology, which assumed that consciousness arises automatically out of experience, and that historians can assemble 'true' (or at least 'better') pictures of the past.

Sometime in the mid-1980s, the story continues, fresh winds of scholarly insight stirred up the musty dust balls of universal domesticity. Coming from several directions, they forced historians of women to rethink their work. Poststructuralist analyses provided a theoretically sophisticated framework for the study of women. Efforts by women of color succeeded in sensitizing white historians of women to diversity. As a result of these developments, gender history began to supplant women's history. Historians seeking knowledge about women now recognize differences between women, problematize the public/private opposition and challenge simplistic epistemologies. If all goes well, they may even manage to incorporate diversity into their research by interrelating gender with race, class and ethnicity.

This is a triumphalist story. It congratulates feminist scholars for trying harder and doing better as the years progress – for incorporating more, for refining their theoretical frameworks and for stretching to encompass difference. The chronology of the narrative is only vaguely specified. Williams, for example, suggests that essentialism dominated for perhaps 'a decade' before 1985. Newman speaks more sweepingly of a generation of historians who established the field of women's history in the 1960s and 1970s by insisting on the inclusion of women.

Seductive though this account is, it does not, in my view, correspond to the facts – to put it in old-fashioned terms. In more modern terms, I want to suggest that this cheery representation of the evolution of feminist historical scholarship is dangerous. The story masks (perhaps represses) alternative narratives that also need to be told. If, as Joan Scott suggests, one of the historian's tasks is to study 'the conflictual processes that produce meanings',[10] we should examine both of these peculiarly interdependent stories. Without such an investigation, we risk being disarmed on the terrain of feminist politics.

In the rest of this chapter I present one of these missing narratives – the one I could not find in Newman's and Williams's accounts but recalled from my own experience. I begin by situating the field of women's history chronologically. As even a cursory examination of the period reveals, what came to be known as the new women's history had no existence in the 1960s and only the rudiments of one during the early 1970s. The field's official beginning could be marked, perhaps, by the First Berkshire Conference on the History of Women, held in 1973. At that historic meeting, scholars, graduate students, independent researchers and activists presented their work to an eager audience of nearly 500 people. I remember the early 1970s as a time of great excitement and expectation, in which a still-expanding feminist activism found a comforting complement in the new scholarship about women. In 1971 and

1972, for example, I participated in a study group whose members included a number of feminists respected today as distinguished pioneers in the field of women's history – Mari Jo Buhle, Ellen DuBois, Linda Gordon, Maureen Greenwald and Meredith Tax, among others.[11] We met to discuss each other's research on such topics as the history of birth control, women and American socialism, the suffrage movement, women workers in early twentieth-century industry, and the life of the labor organizer Mother Jones. While for us women's history was already under way, it took several years for this ground-breaking work to begin to appear in published form. In short, the new women's history got its start in the early 1970s, but only became visible as a scholarly subspecialty in the middle years of the decade.

Contrary to the blurry image projected in the triumphalist narrative, women's history emerged in a specific and highly politicized context. As an intellectual endeavor it was still closely tied to a thriving radical movement of women, which included women who saw themselves as socialist feminists, radical feminists, lesbian feminists, etc.[12] Some of my friends in the women's history study group were probably best known in the early 1970s as leading activists in the women's liberation movement. Many of us sought to make our historical research available in popular pamphlets and magazines as well as scholarly articles and books. Investigation of the past was exciting in part because it recovered lost stories of the forgotten or never-honored women who came before us – activists, victims, ordinary women, all seeming to be heroes of their own lives.

Out of the multifaceted activity of the early 1970s eventually came the first fruits of the new women's history. This is the scholarship the triumphalist narrative patronizes as suffering from methodological and theoretical errors. My alternative story suggests a different picture. In this account, the early practitioners of women's history did not essentialize women and ignore difference. They did not produce a feminism that exalted women's sphere and culture. And they did not operate within a stolidly simple-minded epistemology. What, then, did they do, and how is it that so many today assume the triumphalist version?

An Alternative Account

Intellectual work in the 1960s and early 1970s was conducted against a backdrop of social upheaval wholly unprecedented in the experience of most younger scholars and graduate students. Popular struggles around the globe were seriously disrupting what had seemed to be a stable social order; their outcome appeared still to be uncertain. This history is well known. For the United States, a list of 1960s social movements comes quickly to mind: civil rights, women's rights, the counterculture, Black liberation, antiwar, women's liberation, gay liberation, Native American rights, Puerto Rican independence and others. Joined by a variety of smaller racial/ethnic groups as well as by newly mobilizing movements of the elderly and disabled, these movements were still actively placing their demands on the public agenda in the early 1970s. Meanwhile, national liberation struggles reverberated throughout the Third World, the Chinese Cultural Revolution proffered a model of constant challenge to authority, democratic aspirations swept through Eastern Europe, and movements for self-determination ignited the countries of Western Europe. Tumult on the global level, upheaval at home, demonstrations, teargas and the National Guard perhaps a block away – this context shaped the research on women undertaken at the time. Many of the pioneers in what later became feminist scholarship had been active in the civil rights, student or antiwar movements of the 1960s, or were involved in the women's liberation movement at the decade's end. Even those who sat on or close to the sidelines as they studied women had to be affected by the turbulent social movement of the period. [13]

In this atmosphere, it was hard to ignore categorical differences based on class, race and ethnicity, as well as on age and sexual preference, and there is abundant evidence that the early feminist scholars did not. For example, the well-known collection *Sisterhood Is Powerful* dealt with differences between women by publishing, between other pieces, Fran Beal's 'Double Jeopardy: To Be Black and Female', Jean Tepperman's 'Two Jobs: Women Who Work in Factories', Martha Shelley's 'Notes of a Radical Lesbian' and Zoe Moss's 'It Hurts to Be Alive and Obsolete: The Ageing Woman'. [14] In the anthologies of readings about women, social class was often central, and race and ethnicity were continually acknowledged. [15] Much of the scholarly work in women's history being developed at the time emphasized class and tried also to encompass other kinds of difference, as is evident in the collections *Liberating Women's History, Class, Sex, and the Woman Worker* and *America's Working Women*, the articles published in the first three or four volumes of *Feminist Studies*, and the programs of the First and Second Berkshire Conferences. [16] Then, as now, attempts by white 'middle-class' feminists to acknowledge race and class often fell short. [17] Nonetheless, it must be recognized that the new feminist scholarship sought to address the categorical differences which were the concern of the various social movements of the period.

The new field's commitment to studying a wide spectrum of women's experience was assessed by Carroll Smith-Rosenberg in a review published in 1975. Observing that 'the New Women's History is the product of a complex interaction between the political perspective of the contemporary women's movement and the methodology and focus of the New Social History', Smith-Rosenberg documented the ways historians of women were bringing their feminist sensibilities to bear on the study of women, work and family among 'the inarticulate, the working class, the immigrant and the black'.[18] I would estimate that close to half the research in women's history being conducted at the time concerned non-elite women – working-class women, farm and rural women, African-American women, women in the Third World, women activists in radical movements. Indeed, a review article published in 1982 complained that too much attention was being paid to the history of working-class women and called for more to be directed to the history of women in the professions.[19] Numbers alone do not, of course, reveal the way that class, along with race and ethnicity, constituted the analytical lens through which many of the most influential historians of women looked.

In the early years of women's history, in sum, researchers paid a great deal of attention to differences between women and to women's resistance and public activism. While such questions remained the focus of some scholars' work, a new emphasis on women's culture and on the separate sphere of domesticity swept through the field of women's history in the later 1970s. The existence and some of the evolution of the separate-spheres type of women's history – but not its origins or chronological contours – are documented in fine bibliographical reviews by Nancy Hewitt and Linda Kerber. The scholarly advent of this difference-feminism was perhaps signaled by the publication of Smith-Rosenberg's 'The Female World of Love and Ritual', which brilliantly headed the first issue of *Signs* in 1975.[20]

As before, the larger context undoubtedly influenced both the research undertaken in the later 1970s and its reception. Those years marked the beginning of a long period of economic, political and cultural retrenchment. Many of the social movements of the 1960s collapsed or severely declined. The women's liberation movement survived, but profoundly changed its character, as an energetic cultural feminism arose to celebrate woman's nature and build women's community. In Alice Echols's account, 'a political movement dedicated to eliminating the sex-class system' was replaced by 'a countercultural movement aimed at reversing the cultural valuation of the male and devaluation of the female'.[21] Women's history seems to have been very much in step with these developments, as it moved to explore how female experience is constituted within a distinctive women's space and culture. Like the earlier work, the new approach validated women's lives and gave women agency, but it simultaneously shifted scholarly focus away from structural questions of social organization and power.

On the epistemological front, historians of women in the early 1970s, like many of their counterparts today, found themselves caught in a dilemma. On the one hand, they sought to understand emerging critiques of the philosophical foundations and methodological practices of their discipline; on the other, they were committed to pursuing their research, often already launched within a fairly conventional framework. Questions of relations between knowledge, consciousness and experience are of course not new to philosophy and theory, or to the practice of history. These issues were much discussed in the 1960s and early 1970s – for example, in study groups formed to read and discuss Lukács, Gramsci, Marcuse, the Frankfurt School theorists, Althusser, Poulantzas and others.[22] I remember strenuous critiques of crude materialism, economic determinism and other sorts of reductionism; extended discussions of the relations between structure and agency; and agonizing consideration of the problem of determination in the last instance, or perhaps not at all. The first practitioners of the new women's history were aware of and affected by these various critiques and discussions. It is therefore misleading to claim that their epistemological intentions were constituted simply and unreflectively on the basis of, as Newman puts it, a '[conception] of women's history as an accurate reconstruction of objective experiences'.[23]

Revising the Story

I have described how certain approaches and insights that characterized the first years of the new women's history were displaced from center stage in the later 1970s. Overshadowed by the massive expansion of women's history then under way, the shift took place quietly but not without opposition. That there was a struggle there can be no doubt. Among the traces which remain is the debate on politics and culture in women's history published in *Feminist Studies* in 1980.[24] Here participants considered the relationship between

the concept of women's culture, acknowledged as 'the most significant theoretical formulation' produced by the new women's history,
and the study of women, feminism and social movements. Ellen
DuBois opened the discussion with a challenge to what she saw as a
growing tendency to isolate and romanticize the meaning of
women's culture. Unless women's history kept its focus on feminism
and political questions, she warned, it would lose its commitment to
social change and 'become "depoliticized" and academic in the
worst sense of the word'. Temma Kaplan argued that women's
history must retain its interest in class, for 'it is impossible to speak
of "women's culture" without understanding its variation by class
and ethnic group'. She suggested that 'class analysis of organizations, movements, and cultures in which women are principal participants illuminates female lives in ways that focusing solely upon
women's culture or feminism does not'.[25] Mari Jo Buhle bridged the
poles of the debate with her proposal that the study of women's
culture could illuminate the politics of women's movements, while
Gerda Lerner argued for a politicized notion of women's culture.
Carroll Smith-Rosenberg had the last word. Rejecting the opposition of politics to culture, she presented her approach as the best
way to encompass the 'average' woman's experience. For Smith-
Rosenberg, the important question did not concern politics as much
as the relationship of feminism to the existence of a female world,
ideally a 'rich and vital world of women-identified women'. Her
emphasis on women's 'identification as women', which she called
'the defining characteristic of a female community', represented the
dominant trend in both women's history and the women's liberation
movement at the end of their first decade.[26]

Partially silenced by the turn to the separate-spheres framework
was feminist discussion of a number of critically important issues,
many of them concerning difference, knowledge and power. Among
these, I recall the following as having been of particular interest
during the 1970s: the role of such differences between women as
class, race and sexual preference; the meaning of the special
saliency of race in American history for the study of women; lessons
to be learned from the historical instances of cross-class and cross-
race alliances between women; the relationship, if any, between
Marxism and feminism. Also extensively considered was the problem of the theorization of difference. Many questioned whether
issues of class, race and ethnicity could simply be appended to an
already-established analysis of gender, arguing that categorical
differences had to be theorized in an integrated manner. But what,
specifically, did it mean to analyze these differences as 'inextricably
interrelated'? Most assumed they were to be seen additively, as

comparable or parallel phenomena of more or less equal weight. Some began to suggest the additive approach was inadequate and wondered what might be an alternative theorization. In general, consideration of these various questions had barely started when the shift to a more cultural feminism occurred.[27] By the early 1980s, such concerns had become irrelevant, indeed invisible, for many feminists. Discussion of them likewise almost disappeared.

Not only did the dominant trends within feminist scholarship follow the women's movement into a celebration of women's sphere, but the story has been rewritten – sanitized into the smooth, self-congratulatory fairytale discussed above. For example, in their bibliographical essays, both Hewitt and Kerber document the late-1970s institutionalization of the separate-spheres approach, but say little about women's history in the early 1970s. Thus they leave an impression of continuous development from the 1960s to the early 1980s. Indeed, Kerber explicitly links the 1960s publications of Barbara Welter, Aileen Kraditor and Gerda Lerner, observing that they shared an emphasis on 'the centrality of the metaphor of separate spheres'.[28] Common interest in the metaphor notwithstanding, Lerner's 1969 essay, 'The Lady and the Mill Girl', was read in the early 1970s as a striking challenge to Welter's discussion of 'The Cult of True Womanhood', published in 1966. What distinguished Lerner's article and made it part of the emerging new women's history was precisely its insistence that class matters in the experience of women's sphere.[29] For those embarking on the study of the history of women, Lerner's essay served as an important confirmation of the utility of taking class as a fundamental analytical category. But for Kerber, rereading the work nearly two decades later, attention to such inconvenient discontinuities seems unnecessary. Focusing on historians' interest in separate spheres, she can move seamlessly from true womanhood in the mid-1960s to women's culture a decade later.

With the discontinuities suppressed and the story revised in this way, those of us who were there at the beginning are astonished to find ourselves criticized for a conceptual framework whose hegemony in the new women's history we distrusted and in some measure challenged.[30] First came astonishment – and then questions. The meaning of the reconstructed narrative needs to be scrutinized. In particular, I would pose the questions Williams and Newman ask so appropriately in their papers. Why is this rewritten narrative enjoying such a 'stunning popularity'? How was this particular feminist discourse of the late 1980s produced? Why did it emerge when it did? Where and in what cultural forms has it been represented?

I would also want to ask some questions about the reappearance of difference on the feminist – and, indeed, the social – agenda. An intense interest in multiculturalism and diversity characterizes contemporary feminist scholarship, and it marks curricular debates more generally as well. Especially noteworthy is the role of African-American, Latina and Asian-American feminist scholars in furthering discussion and research. This renewal of interest in difference is an important and very welcome development, and it entails a struggle over terms and meaning that is essentially political. Multiple discourses can center on diversity, not all of them compatible with what feminists and people of color might intend. Thus I am simultaneously optimistic and nervous about the widespread acceptance of diversity discourse. And I wonder also about some of the motivations behind projects to 'balance' the curriculum, or 'value diversity'. Along with others, I ask how today's notions of diversity differ from early 1970s understandings of difference. Is the politics of diversity analogous to what used to be called antisexist/antipatriarchal/antiracist politics?

To some extent, it seems to me, the term diversity is functioning as a code name for the resuscitation of an official pluralism which ultimately denies the hierarchies associated with difference. That is, the way diversity is often promulgated and understood can serve to mask the specific historical character of collective oppression. Where formerly we were all expected to dissolve our specificity in the melting pot, now we are said to retain some hard core of cultural identity as a tessera in the gorgeous mosaic. Either way – whether considered one ingredient among others in the social soup, or one flinty chip among others in the social mosaic – the distinctiveness of our historically constituted subordinate positions within various social hierarchies appears to be lost. Paradoxically, this loss is as palpable in current celebrations of the wonders of a generalized diversity as it was in the just-abandoned exaltation of women's sphere. In both cases, an enthusiastic homogenization deflects attention from power and the stubborn harshness of particular oppressions.

If diversity and the gorgeous mosaic do not move as far beyond the melting pot as some had hoped, we should probably call a halt to our cheerful triumphalism. Not that feminists must abandon diversity; rather, we need to figure out just what we want to mean by it. Our interpretations probably span a range, and they may also differ from those produced from within other positions in the social structure. We should, in short, clarify our notions of a scholarship – and a politics – of difference.[31] As I have suggested here, one important step in this process is diligently to investigate the diverse meanings in our own recent history.[32]

110

9 BEYOND EQUALITY: SOME FEMINIST QUESTIONS

In the 1980s, equality became an object of feminist contention. This was a startling development, for equal treatment in law and public policy had long been the principal goal of second-wave feminism. Although two decades of activism had enabled American women to move closer to the goal, much remained to be accomplished. The Equal Rights Amendment was not yet ratified. Courts addressed sex discrimination only up to a point. Occupational and income gaps between women and men were as obvious as ever. For most feminists, the equality agenda of the 1960s was still on the table.

Thus it was unexpected when some feminists began to critique equality. The discussion centered on maternity in the workplace. Given the unique character of motherhood, the argument went, being treated the same as men did not always produce fair results for women. While pregnant, women employees have special needs that their employers should acknowledge by granting lighter duties, rest periods, time to visit the doctor and the like. At childbirth, they must of course be given time off. Later, they may need extra leave to attend to a sick child. Faced with the specificities of women's lives, equality suddenly appeared inadequate as a goal of social policy.

The critique of equality did not come entirely as a surprise to me. As a participant in the Southern civil rights movement of the early 1960s, I had felt first hand the tension between demanding equality and wanting justice. The freedom struggle projected a vision of equality as human rights that went well beyond legal sameness. When its double commitment to formal equality and the beloved community migrated into the women's liberation movement at the end of the decade, I followed along with many others.

My efforts to develop Marxist-feminist theory had also alerted me to the contradictions of equality. Although the socialist tradition was said to be contemptuous of equality, in writing Marxism and the

111

Oppression of Women *I discovered that the canonical texts offer a more complicated account.*[1] *I argued, moreover, that denial of equality is a fundamental feature of women's situation, constituted from within the workings of capitalism as a mode of production.*

In this chapter, I consider the feminist challenge to equality. Because the essay owes its existence to a presentation at a 1993 conference on Feminism and Legal Theory, the audience is presumed to be the feminist legal community. But the arguments I offer have wider application. On the one hand, I examine the critique of equality developed in the 1980s. What are we to think when equality no longer seems adequate to our vision of justice? On the other hand, I address the problem of theorizing difference and diversity in the 1990s. If we discard the liberal belief that all persons are essentially the same, what then?

Introduction

For some time, traditional assumptions about the meaning of 'rights' and 'equality' have been the object of critique in the legal community. The most trenchant questions come from radical-minded academics whose roots are in the social movements of the 1960s. Critical Legal Studies scholars dispute the practical usefulness and theoretical integrity of rights claims.[2] Feminist legal scholars doubt the ability of equality jurisprudence to address the subordination of women. Given persisting structural inequalities, they observe, the hard-won achievements of earlier feminist activism now seem inadequate, even dangerous to the interests of women.[3]

Litigation concerning pregnancy in the workplace revealed the problematic character of equality with particular clarity. In the 1980s, feminists divided over the merits of statutes making disability leave available to pregnant workers even when their temporarily disabled co-workers were denied the benefit. Such female-specific policies attempted to foster sex equality through the provision of dissimilar treatment. Although the United States Supreme Court affirmed the validity of pregnancy disability leave statutes in *California Federal* v. *Guerra* (1987), the controversy – known as the equality-versus-difference debate – continues to haunt feminist thinking. The issue of reproductive hazards in the workplace, for example, is generating in the 1990s disagreements quite similar to those about pregnancy leave a decade ago.[4]

Why can't feminists get beyond equality-versus-difference

dilemmas? One reason is the US legal system, which forces us to consider policy on its terms rather than ours. But another reason is that we haven't paid careful enough attention to how the issues are constructed. In this paper I resist the temptation to rehearse the equality-versus-difference opposition yet again, and instead take it apart. Once disassembled and examined, the pieces no longer seem to come from a coherent entity.

Equality versus Difference?

The conventional construction of the problem of pregnancy policy has been in terms of an opposition between two positions, equal treatment and special treatment. A careful reading shows, however, that a spectrum of theoretical perspectives accompanies each pole of the supposed dichotomy. In the next two sections, I examine these positions more closely, demonstrating their range and diversity.[5]

For the sake of clarity, my survey of the various positions in the debate discards the equal-treatment/special-treatment terminology that dominated it. Instead, I use a version of Christine Littleton's conceptualization of the opposition in terms of symmetrical and asymmetrical approaches to gender difference.[6] Littleton's language of symmetry and asymmetry is appropriate for describing the strategies advocated by participants in the pregnancy policy debates, but it is less apt as a means of differentiating their theoretical positions, at least partly because it still connotes the dualism of its predecessors. In my discussion I therefore modify Littleton's conceptualization. As schematically represented in Figure 1 (overleaf), I use the terms symmetry and asymmetry to designate strategic orientations only. Asymmetrists are those who support female-specific policies; symmetrists are those who oppose such policies, arguing instead that carefully designed gender-neutral policies can best meet women's needs. It should be noted that I use the term gender-neutral strictly to refer to the legal form of law and policy. As will become evident, some gender-neutral policies are normatively male while others are gender-inclusive, even diversity-inclusive.[7]

Symmetrists

I start with the equal-treatment position – the symmetrists. The symmetrist approach to gender difference has played a central role in second-wave feminism. The theoretical implications of the

Theoretical Position	Strategic Orientation
Assimilation	
Androgyny	*Symmetrist*
Genderlessness	
Special rights	
Dominance	
Accommodation	*Assymetrist*
Acceptance	

Figure 1

strategy have received relatively little attention, however. Symmetrists justify formally gender-neutral policies mainly on practical rather than theoretical grounds, focusing on institutional constraints and strategic dangers. Within their arguments, at least three distinct theoretical positions can be discerned: assimilation, androgyny and genderlessness. [8]

Assimilationism is the traditional liberal approach to social recognition of categorical differences, and it is the one that courts most easily understand. In this view, race and gender, like eye color, are characteristics that should not be allowed to matter. Individuals who are similarly situated with respect to a particular purpose should be treated alike, regardless of group differences – real or imagined, biologically or culturally constituted. Applied to women, assimilationism assumes that women really are, or given the opportunity could be, just like men in all important respects. Gender specificities of course exist, but they should not be permitted to make a difference.

Because assimilationism constructs women as fundamentally the same as men, it has difficulty incorporating the physical differences associated with procreation. Traditionally, it set sex-based physiological differences aside, as in the nineteenth-century liberal-feminist focus on equal rights and opportunities in the public sphere. More recently, assimilationism has addressed physical sex differences by making a close analogy or equation of female-specific traits and general characteristics – converting pregnancy, for example, into a temporary disability. In this way, women's needs are validated as being exactly like those of men. Whether physiological sex difference is ignored for the particular purposes at hand or converted to supposedly universal terms, assimilationism takes men as the norm.[9] The role of social policy, for assimilationists, is to eliminate obstacles that block women's ability to participate in society's institutions on the same basis as men. No structural changes to those institutions are necessary.

An assimilationist position was implicit in the efforts of the feminist policy community in the 1960s and 1970s. Campaigns to overturn the legacy of protectionism, for instance, usually reflected an assimilationist view. Early twentieth-century female-specific measures seemed to be based on unwarranted assumptions of women's global difference, and feminists fought for women to have the same rights and access as men in all areas of social life. At a time when women were treated unfavorably with respect to education, training, promotion and basic citizenship rights, the equation of equality with same treatment appeared to make sense.

Assimilationism is not the only theoretical position associated with the symmetrist approach to gender difference. Symmetrist participants in the pregnancy policy debate have frequently embraced an equality vision they call androgyny. These legal androgynists – for example, Wendy Williams and Nadine Taub – use analogy to deal with the stubborn specificity of sex-unique traits, as do assimilationists. But they shift the object of their analogies from physiological characteristics to persons. That is, they invoke analogies not in order to convert sex-specific physical conditions to a supposedly universal basis, but to draw out the commonalities in the lives of differently sexed persons.

Androgyny and assimilationism offer different analyses and have divergent practical implications. In the case of pregnancy, for instance, the assimilationist likening of pregnancy to disability obliterates the specificity of women's needs. By contrast, androgyny constructs pregnant women as different from their co-workers, but with analogously special needs when temporarily disabled. In this way it can acknowledge the special character of pregnancy. More generally, androgyny requires 'a redefinition of what a typical employee is that encompasses both sexes'. The work environment will therefore have to be restructured. It is not enough to drop the obvious barriers to women becoming pilots, firefighters and professors; airplane cockpits, firefighting equipment and lecture podiums must be redesigned. In this way, the androgynist use of the equality framework can 'overcome the definition of the prototypical worker as male and ... promote an integrated – and androgynous – prototype'. [10]

The 1978 Pregnancy Discrimination Act is conceptualized in legal androgynist terms. Rather than defining pregnancy as a disability, the Act requires employers to make analogies between their employees. If able to work, pregnant and non-pregnant employees must be treated the same; likewise, workers temporarily disabled by reason of pregnancy or for other reasons can expect the same treatment. Employers are thus prohibited from discriminating against their pregnant employees; for example, by forcing them to take leave or denying them benefits available to other temporarily disabled workers. Moreover, an employer whose inadequate disability leave policy has a disparate impact on pregnant employees, could be required to redesign benefits to provide not just pregnancy leave but more adequate disability leave for all workers. In this way, the employer is forced 'to modify the male-defined workplace so as to encompass the experience of both sexes. [This approach] encourages an androgynous rather than male model in the workplace'. [11]

A third symmetrist position, which I call genderlessness, has recently been proposed by philosopher Susan Moller Okin. In her view, 'a just future would be one without gender'. As in assimilationism, a person's sex should ideally be no more relevant than eye color in shaping his or her social experience. But Okin recognizes, as assimilationists do not, that a massive restructuring of social institutions is required to achieve the gender-free society. She therefore proposes an array of practical measures, familiar to contemporary feminists: parental leave, subsidized day care, flexible working hours, more equitable post-divorce parenting arrangements, etc. In the long run, Okin argues, 'gender-free families' and the 'genderless society' will provide the best context for the development of human capacities and the realization of social justice. [12]

Asymmetrists

Assimilation and androgyny are the two theoretical positions most frequently used to justify symmetrist strategies. They are generally rejected by feminist legal academics, however, and genderlessness is not likely to prove any more popular. Asymmetrists, who dominate legal scholarship,[13] tend to dismiss all equal-treatment positions as irredeemably simplistic applications of formal equality. In Lucinda Finley's formulation, equality doctrine 'inherently assumes that the goal is assimilation to an existing standard without questioning the desirability of that standard and thus it limits the debate to what policies will best achieve the assimilation'.[14] Asymmetrists' theoretical efforts focus on developing analyses of how gender makes a difference and what to do about it. Four theoretical positions justifying female-specific policies can be distinguished in the feminist legal literature: special rights, dominance, accommodation and acceptance.

The special rights perspective was articulated in 1980 by Elizabeth Wolgast. Linking a critique of equality thinking to a rejection of liberal individualism, Wolgast argues against the notion of androgyny. For her, human beings are in essence a divided species and 'justice requires men and women to be treated differently'. Real differences between women and men can be documented, she claims, in their behavior, psychology and moral reasoning as well as physiology. As mothers, women have special needs that require the installation of a system of special rights alongside equal rights:

> The two kinds of rights, equal and differential (or special), work very differently. With regard to an equal right, taking a person's individual qualities into account may constitute discrimination. But with special rights, they must be taken into account, for these rights are based on human differences.

Just as ramps enable persons in wheelchairs to have equal access to buildings and public spaces, the provision of special measures to address women's needs promotes a real sexual equality. Only on this basis can women 'make their own distinctive contribution to the culture and society'.[15]

Wolgast, a philosopher, developed the argument for special rights through analysis of United States Supreme Court decisions concerning gender, and her scrutiny of equality thinking was extremely influential in the feminist legal community. Her expansive characterization of special rights comes dangerously close to traditional protectionism, however, as many immediately observed. Because would-be advocates of the special rights position have 'their feet precariously planted on the slippery slope of judicial stereotyping',[16] few participants in the equal-treatment/special-treatment debate actually espouse Wolgast's argument. Rather,

117

like assimilationism, the special rights position has mainly functioned in the controversy as a point of departure.[17]

The dominance perspective is at the opposite end from the special rights model on the spectrum of positions held by legal asymmetrists. Its central premise is an absolute rejection of the notions of difference and equality. In this view, pioneered by Catharine MacKinnon, difference is as chimerical a basis for the analysis of gender asymmetry as equality, for both are defined by male power. 'The question of equality ... is at root a question of hierarchy, which – as power succeeds in constructing social perception and social reality – derivatively becomes a categorical distinction, a difference'.[18] Feminists mired in the special-treatment/equal-treatment debate fail to see that the two positions are 'two different versions of the male standard. If you see gender as a hierarchy ... you realize that the options of either being the same as men or being different from men are just two ways of having men as your standard'.[19] By contrast, the dominance perspective situates the issue of concern not as women's difference, but as their domination by men. The goal is not to achieve equality but to address hierarchy directly in order to end women's subordination. The dominance perspective suggests that policies and practices be evaluated according to whether they reinforce or reduce the domination of women by men.

With its radical challenge to the conventions of legal thinking, the dominance perspective has been pivotal in the development of feminist legal theory. Proponents of the position have not, however, been able to force the legal system to respond to their challenge. While feminist dominance theorists refine their analyses, the law continues to look at women in terms of sameness and difference. In Deborah Rhode's evaluation, 'the sources of this theory's strengths are also the sources of its limitations. ... As a foundation for an alternative legal framework, dominance paradigms are too often theoretically reductive and strategically counterproductive'. Essentialist and deterministic as theory, dominance has also proven unreliable as a guide to the formulation of policy.[20]

The asymmetrist approaches most commonly endorsed in feminist legal scholarship are accommodation and acceptance. Like the dominance perspective, these orientations shift the emphasis 'from gender difference to gender disadvantage' – that is, to the adverse consequences of gender difference in women's lives.[21] Unlike dominance, these perspectives permit feminist policy proposals to be formulated within more conventional legal terms. Both the accommodation and the acceptance approaches justify sex-specific measures in appropriately bounded circumstances on

118

the basis of certain differences between women and men. They diverge, however, in their delineation of the boundaries of relevant gender difference.

The accommodation perspective posits a dualism in the treatment of women that is strictly limited. It endorses same treatment as the policy standard in most situations, but proposes that narrowly defined female-specific measures be used to accommodate physiological sex differences. Ann Scales first described the approach in her 1980–1 discussion of 'incorporationism'. Rejecting Wolgast's notion of special rights as too broad, Scales suggests that 'women should be recognized to have rights different from men only insofar as pregnancy and breastfeeding, the only aspects of childbearing and childrearing completely unique to women, are directly concerned'.[22] Sylvia Law likewise proposes that special measures pertaining to pregnancy and breastfeeding be evaluated using MacKinnon's dominance standard; all other gender specificities are to be addressed by gender-neutral means.[23] Herma Hill Kay suggests that conventional equality analysis cannot be applied in the presence of real physiological differences. Her 'episodic' approach would acknowledge biological difference by validating some sex-specific treatment of pregnant, nursing or menstruating women, as well as of men who rape.[24]

The accommodationist position – the notion that special treatment is valid when used to accommodate 'real', that is physiologically based, difference – has occasionally been acknowledged in public policy. One example is the federal government's Special Supplement Food Program for Women, Infants and Children, known as WIC, which provides nutritional supplements to pregnant and nursing mothers, infants and young children; special treatment to address the needs of the physically disabled is another. In 1987, the United States Supreme Court used accommodationist reasoning in *California Federal* v. *Guerra*, the decision that affirmed pregnancy disability leave legislation.[25]

The acceptance perspective has been advanced by Christine Littleton. Where accommodation validates female-specific measures on an extremely limited basis, acceptance throws the difference net more broadly, encompassing cultural as well as biological sex differences. The goal is to achieve 'equal acceptance' for male and female activities and attributes as they are currently constructed. The acceptance position targets the unjust consequences of difference regardless of its source. 'Whether the gender "difference" is seen as biological or social, it must be rendered costless in order to achieve true equality'.[26]

Like the special rights perspective, acceptance proposes that women and men be treated differently where the asymmetry of their lives requires it. Unlike special rights, acceptance recognizes the need for a systematic procedure to determine the appropriateness and limits of sex-specific measures. Littleton's method is to identify complementary ways that women and men 'stand in asymmetrical positions to a particular social institution'.[27] Where society encodes difference in such 'gender complements', an equalizing analysis is to be applied. In the employment context, for example, socially 'male' and 'female' skills should be equally valued and compensated. With respect to pregnancy, women who become mothers and men who become fathers constitute gender complements and ought to be able to choose to combine parenthood and employment to the same extent. More generally, Littleton suggests that society constructs warriors and mothers as gender complements: 'Both occupations involve a lot of unpleasant work, along with a real sense of commitment to a cause beyond oneself that is culturally gussied up and glamorized culturally to cover up the unpleasantness involved. Both involve danger and possible death'. Perhaps, she speculates, society ought to compensate mothers in the same way as soldiers, or make motherhood an unofficial qualification for running for political office.[28]

The theory of equality as acceptance is attractive, for it promises to go beyond the limits of the accommodation position without recreating the difficulties of Wolgast's special rights approach. A number of feminist legal scholars produce work that can be placed within the acceptance framework, even if they do not adopt Littleton's methodology for evaluating sex-specific measures. Finley, for example, suggests 'responsibility analysis' should supplement equality analysis 'where women appear to be truly different from men – in their capacity to become pregnant and their traditional relegation to the sphere of childrearing'.[29] She is thus able to recommend an array of female-specific policies to address the cultural as well as physiological specificity of women.

The asymmetrist positions just discussed are vulnerable to criticism based on strategic considerations. As symmetrists often point out, female-specific measures can easily be converted into pretexts for the disadvantageous treatment of women. Affirmations of cultural and biological sex difference have risky ideological and theoretical implications as well. Littleton herself comments that 'matching gendered complements in order to equalize across cultural differences may sound like marching directly into the valley of the stereotypes'.[30]

120

Difference

The equality-versus-difference debate has been assumed to construct equality and difference as polar opposites, offering only two
policy options. Either one supports equality theory and a same-
treatment strategy; or one affirms woman's difference in order to
endorse female-specific treatment on some limited basis. Contrary
to this assumption, the discussion in the previous section demonstrates that most positions in the debate actually theorize an equality that acknowledges difference. Even assimilationism, the
staunchest in its commitment to a notion of women as essentially
the same as men, does not deny difference. Rather, it views gender
distinctions as characteristics that are present but should not
matter. Three of the asymmetrist perspectives – special rights,
accommodation and acceptance – as well as androgyny in the symmetrist category, incorporate female specificity more wholeheart-
edly. That is, they offer concepts of gender equality that depend, at
bottom, on an affirmation of female difference. In this way they
seek to shape policies that can better serve women by retaining
elements of gender specificity alongside or within the equality
framework established in the 1960s and 1970s.

Freed from the simplifications of the equality/difference dichotomy, the various perspectives developed in feminist legal
scholarship can be seen more clearly. In particular, it becomes
obvious that they sometimes reproduce the dilemmas from which
their creators had hoped to escape. Several difficulties, all pertaining to the representation of difference, stand out in particular: the
use of essentialist notions of difference; insufficient recognition of
the pervasiveness of difference; and concepts of difference and
diversity that focus on individuals.

Essentialist understandings of woman's difference permeate symmetrist and asymmetrist accounts in a variety of ways. The dualism
of the accommodationist approach to social policy presumes, for
example, an essential normalcy punctuated by occasional deviance.
Same treatment is to be the general rule, but sex-specific measures
can be used to accommodate real physiological characteristics. The
two tracks imply two standards. On the one hand, conventional
equality norms are to apply in most situations; on the other, special
sex-specific norms can be invoked on a limited basis. Accommodationism thus posits an opposition between 'normal' persons, the
standard to whom equality rules apply, and (temporarily) 'abnormal'
persons, for whom special measures are necessary.

Accommodationism's two-track approach unthinkingly resurrects formulations proposed two decades earlier. In a pathbreaking 1971 article on the Equal Rights Amendment, feminist legal strategists allowed that gender-specific legislation concerning sex-unique physical traits is permissible as long as it is 'closely, directly and narrowly confined to the unique physical characteristic'.[31] Of course, as Sylvia Law observes, the authors of this article under-estimated the centrality of the issue of female-specific treatment, and proposed no independent principle to justify special meas-ures.[32] But their argument that female-specific policies can be consistent with the equality framework actually reflects a two-track normative essentialism that is well established in American law. Traditional jurisprudence quite comfortably endorses broadly neutral rules applying to all alongside a carefully delimited set of exceptions.[33]

Many feminist legal scholars deploy essentialist notions of differ-ence in another way when they focus their concerns solely on gen-der. Whether theorized in terms of assimilation, androgyny, special rights, dominance, accommodation or acceptance, difference is repeatedly constructed as exclusively grounded in gender. For instance, actors are depicted as male or female but somehow lack-ing other defining characteristics. Where race and class are men-tioned, little effort is made to incorporate them theoretically. Such accounts articulate an unmodulated opposition of female to male, and disregard other kinds of categorical specificity. Strenuously condemning the dichotomous formulations haunting the equality-versus-difference debate, participants do not see the ways in which their own work reproduces an essentialist focus on gender.

Feminist legal scholarship only rarely acknowledges what has elsewhere become a commonplace observation: the pervasiveness of difference throughout social life. In their inattention to the full range of human heterogeneity, feminist legal academics have been oddly out of step with a great deal of recent work in other dis-ciplines. Since the early 1980s, the scholarly community has become increasingly sensitive to the diversity of social experience. Such characteristics as race, ethnicity, class, gender, sexuality, age and ability are now recognized as always present and active. For example, if other distinctive characteristics go unmentioned in a study centered on gender, it is understood that they only appear to be effaced. The omission actually signals an underlying assumption that the women and men of concern are white, middle-class, English-speaking, heterosexual, able-bodied and so forth. Silence on these aspects of being does not obliterate them as dimensions of difference. On the contrary: silence eloquently privileges what is already hegemonic and thereby reinforces hierarchy.[34]

Theorizing Diversity: History

Recent research in a number of fields not only recognizes diversity, it also attempts to address it theoretically. Feminist theorists have sought an integrated framework that can respond to the specificity of all differences. Some suggest that such a diversity-inclusive framework may require a radical decentering of sexual difference. Here again, feminist legal scholarship has fallen short, focusing mainly on gender and drawing on a limited range of theory. The work of Carol Gilligan has been one important source, and that of Catharine MacKinnon another. Where Gilligan embraces gender difference, MacKinnon rejects it. But both ignore categorical specificities other than gender.[35]

The task of theorizing diversity is, of course, extremely difficult. Significant progress has been made, particularly in the last decade, and most especially by feminists of color. Living at the structural intersection of the most salient categorical oppressions – those based on race and gender as well as, often, class – women of color are well placed to produce a knowledge that encompasses diversity. At least since the late 1960s they have sought to theorize the position of women of color in a way that is inclusive of a broad range of specificities.[36]

One of the earliest contributions to modern Black feminist thought was made by Frances Beal, at the time a coordinator of the Black Women's Liberation Committee, affiliated to the Student Nonviolent Coordinating Committee (SNCC). In 'Double Jeopardy: To Be Black and Female', first published in 1969, Beal argues that Black women are oppressed as both women and Blacks in a context dominated by capitalist exploitation.[37] The article, much discussed and widely reprinted, constituted a starting point within women's liberationist theory, from which developed more complex understandings of the ways categorical oppressions intersect. In particular, Beal's formulation in terms of double jeopardy was quickly reworked into a notion of triple oppression based on race, class and sex. Whether envisioned as a double or a triple jeopardy, the underlying model being proposed was insufficiently specified. It conceptualized the oppressions as comparable or parallel phenomena of more or less equal weight, but it did not address the dynamics of how they related to one another. Simultaneously distinct and inextricably intertwined, sex, race and class factors were assumed simply to accumulate in an additive manner.

By the late 1970s, some feminists were expressing discomfort with the inadequacies of a theoretical model that paralleled race, class and sex.[38] What, they wondered, did it mean to analyze oppressions as inextricably intertwined? How were the inter-relationships to be theorized? In contrast to the dominant trends in the mostly white radical women's movement of the period, which was emphasizing sisterhood and the common experience of women,[39] feminists of color continued to insist on the special character of women's lives as members of particular groups. At the same time, they launched a search for a more adequate theorization.

The 1980s saw a variety of efforts to modify the additive (or interaction) model while preserving its respect for the diversity of women. Sociologist Deborah King, for example, proposed a more interactive theorization in terms of multiple, rather than double, jeopardy. Psychologist Aida Hurtado argued that the issue was less the interrelationship of sex, race and class factors than the relative positioning of particular oppressed groups with respect to white men. Anthropologist Karen Brodkin Sacks suggested a reconceptualization of class that would encompass race and gender diversity within notions of membership in a community. Sociologist Patricia Hill Collins explored how an Afrocentric feminist epistemology might reveal a many-leveled matrix of domination.[40] Other efforts to theorize race, class, and gender in a nonadditive manner moved even more radically away from mechanical notions of interacting factors.[41]

The investigations just outlined took the relationship of race and gender as their central concern. An analogous yet largely independent project attempted to theorize women's oppression in terms of an integrated system of class and sex stratification. Initiated during the late 1960s by socialist feminists in the women's liberation movement, this work sought radically to transform socialist theory to encompass women's oppression. Theorists began by proposing various sorts of dual-systems theories; arguing, for instance, that women's oppression can be explained in terms of parallel mechanisms of capitalism and patriarchy. By the late 1970s, the mechanistic and additive character of dual-systems thinking was being subjected to severe criticism. As with the feminist theorists interested in race, a search began for a more unified theorization of the relationship between group oppressions.[42]

This brief survey demonstrates that efforts to theorize categorical difference have constituted a line of feminist inquiry for more than two decades. Rooted originally in the oppositional social movements of the 1960s and 1970s, the work was soon also undertaken by feminists located in the academy. To suggest, as many contemporary commentators do, that 'race only posed itself as an urgent issue to [feminist scholars] in the last couple of years' is therefore misleading.[43] The common assumption that feminism first confronted diversity in the 1980s diminishes a complex and multifaceted history.[44] Triumphalist in its implications, the simplified narrative reflects the view from a particular position. From a different vantage point, recent feminist interest in diversity appears as the discovery by white academics in elite universities of an important issue already established as an object of scholarly interest within second-wave feminism. No doubt fueled by the arrival of feminists of color to positions in institutions of higher education, the expanding attention to diversity also responds to developments in society at large. All too often, however, the questions are posed without acknowledgment of earlier attempts both to ask and to answer them.

Theorizing Diversity: Problems

In one way or another, diversity has long been an issue for feminism, with the recent heightened attention marking a new and exciting stage. As with difference, the meaning of diversity is contested and requires scrutiny. Some facets are already under examination. For example, hard though it has turned out to be to transcend dualistic accounts of diversity by means of a nonadditive analysis, the importance of doing so is now widely acknowledged. Two other issues are less frequently identified as problems: the representation of difference in relation to social hierarchy and the conceptualization of diversity.

Discussions of difference and diversity do not always pay attention to hierarchies established through structural relations of power. When, for instance, diversity is celebrated as a rich reflection of human individuality and social variation, but little mention is made of any associated penalties or oppression, power is denied. By simultaneously acknowledging cultural heterogeneity and remaining silent about the ways different social groups are positioned within a hierarchical order, such celebrations mask domination. A few commentators have pointed to this problem. Historian Linda Gordon, for example, argues that 'the concept of "difference" ... implies a pluralist multiplicity of stories that benignly coexist or interact; it may obscure relations of inequality, domination, and even exploitation among women'. Likewise, literary critic Hazel Carby suggests that the language of difference and diversity is currently being used to marginalize analysis of structures of dominance.[45]

More rarely recognized as a problematic issue is the question of the meaning of diversity as a concept. Commentators ordinarily do not make a distinction between specificity as a characteristic of individuals and as a group phenomenon, often using 'difference' or 'diversity' to refer to both.[46] In many accounts, specificity at the level of groups – which could be distinguished by such terms as categorical diversity or group diversity – is represented as a simple extension of characteristics attached to individuals: sex, race, age, affectional preference and so forth. Diversity is thus understood to refer simultaneously to the existence of differences between individuals and between collections of individuals sharing particular characteristics – for example, women, men, African-Americans, whites, children, adults, lesbians and gays, heterosexuals and so forth. Group diversity is conceptualized, in other words, as a series of aggregated individual specificities, often arranged in bipolar pairs; individuals appear to be constituted, improbably, as members of many such groups. What is missing from this picture is an adequate account of social structure on the one hand, and of identity on the other.

In sum, categorical diversity is often thought of as individual specificity crystallized, writ large and innocent of power. This elision of levels has the political correlates flagged by Carby, Gordon and others. That is, once diversity is stripped of its special character as a power-laden and irreducibly heterogeneous group phenomenon, it becomes possible to put difference at the service of an unoffending pluralism.

In the legal arena, Martha Minow's influential effort to theorize difference provides a good example of the consequences of disregarding diversity's variegated and structural character.[47] Minow wishes to respect the broad range of diversity, but her account is undermined by its inadequate construction of the concept. Despite her intentions, she tends to reduce human heterogeneity to a single, supposedly characteristic opposition – embodied in her repeated positing of children and the physically and mentally disabled as oppression's paradigmatic victims. For Minow, the injuries of difference are located in processes of interpersonal labeling and stigmatization. Difference becomes an issue of relations between competent adults and incompetent, voiceless, dependent individuals who do not belong to historically constituted communities. Diversity is represented not only as invariant in form but also as an individualistic phenomenon that is largely independent of culture and history – indeed, a product of the irrational human tendency to stigmatize individual others as different.

Minow's policy suggestions envision transforming the perspective of the individuals involved in stigmatization processes. Once they understand difference to be a function of the stigmatizing relation-ship between 'normals' and 'abnormals', connection can be estab-lished and disadvantageous treatment halted. For example, the law has traditionally been expected to adjudicate on the merits of providing special treatment for disabled persons versus mainstream-ing them. Minow rejects the choice, proposing that the standards of normalcy be shifted instead. Rather than deciding between the harms of separation and the difficulties of integration, the law can foster a relational solution. In the case of deaf children, for instance, hearing children can learn sign language, thereby trans-forming the classroom into a little commonwealth of sensitive communicators. Not surprisingly, examples of race or sex stigmati-zation are virtually absent from Minow's text, for these phenomena pose disruptive questions concerning social power and categorical subordination. With the discussion centered on differences of age and ability, structural hierarchy and group specificity vanish in a cornucopia of liberal goodwill.

It isn't easy to see how a more adequate theorization of diversity can be developed. Certain steps could be taken to clarify the issues. In the first place, diversity should be conceptually distinguished from difference as a term associated with groups; assumptions that map individual specificities into group diversity can thus be prob-lematized. Second, diversity must be located within a structural understanding of social organization as involving power and hier-archy – at least insofar as diversity is characteristic of today's complex societies. Third, diversity should be recognized as relent-lessly heterogeneous; for example, sex, race and class cannot simply be paralleled with one another as if they were comparable phenom-ena. Fourth, the construction of identity needs to be understood as an ongoing, inherently contested process of negotiation across many divides.

In short, feminist legal scholarship has only begun to confront the complexity of the concepts implicated in the construction of the opposition of difference to equality. In this essay I have shown that the equality-versus-difference debate poses a series of difficult questions largely overlooked in the literature. A more satisfactory response to the policy and theoretical dilemmas re-quires that these questions be addressed.[48]

10 CONSIDERING DIFFERENCE: THE CASE OF THE FAMILY AND MEDICAL LEAVE ACT OF 1993

The questions feminists posed in the 1980s about equality have policy as well as theoretical implications.[1] Given the sometimes inadequate results of treating women the same as men, some feminists disparage the use of formally gender-neutral measures. They suggest that female-specific policies – for example, pregnancy disability leave – can better meet the needs of women.

In this chapter, I challenge the assumption that only two options are available for designing policies for women. Using the Family and Medical Leave Act of 1993 as my example, I argue that a new kind of policy thinking, which I name differential consideration, better represents feminist aspirations for the 1990s. Implicitly, my claim is also that differential consideration policies at this time best embody the materialist feminist critique.

Introduction

The 1993 Family and Medical Leave Act (FMLA) has been widely hailed as a significant step forward in US social policy. For the first time, American women's need for maternity leave is being addressed by national legislation. The statute requires employers to provide time off for employees for a variety of reasons, including pregnancy, childbirth and care of the newborn.[2] Leave is unpaid, but job- and benefit-protected. Because the legislation applies only to firms of a certain size, no more than 60 per cent of the workforce is covered.

Meager though the FMLA's benefits actually are when measured by international standards,[3] politicians and the media claim its passage constitutes a sea change. At last the notion that the

128

state should help its citizens meld family and work responsibilities has been put on the US policy agenda. In Vice-President Albert Gore's words, 'American families will no longer have to choose between their families and their jobs'.[4]

US feminists likewise welcomed the new legislation. Some, however, added words of caution. During the eight years it was under congressional consideration, the FMLA attracted substantial feminist criticism. Its benefits were dismissed as too limited to be useful to those most in need. Its gender neutrality was viewed as problematic, given the particular needs of women and the structural realities of the US workplace. Its ideological implications were characterized as assimilationist – constructing women as just like men in all relevant respects – and thereby insensitive to women's difference.

In this essay I examine the feminist critique of the FMLA. In particular I challenge the common assumption that the statute's gender-neutral legal form necessarily entails an assimilationist vision. Far from being assimilationist, the FMLA takes account of special needs. I argue that despite its substantive limitations, the legislation represents an important new direction in US social policy.

The Critique

Two charges exemplify feminists' misgivings about the Family and Medical Leave Act. The first targets its supposed disregard of the gender specialness of pregnancy and motherhood. Critics note that pregnancy is a physiologically normal process. As physician and feminist activist Wendy Chavkin puts it, pregnancy 'is not an illness. Rather, it is a unique condition that may be accompanied by special needs and sometimes by illness'.[5] The FMLA's treatment of pregnancy as if it were a medical problem like any other is thus, in the critics' view, inappropriate. The legislation also ignores, they suggest, the unique social contribution of mothers, who are responsible for nurturing society's next generation. By taking pregnancy to be akin to a disability, the FMLA fails to consider women's special difference and mothers' special role.

The second charge focuses on social class. Along with conservatives who have tagged the FMLA a 'yuppie bill', feminist critics claim the legislation will mainly cover women with professional and other high-status careers. Working-class women – the vast majority of women workers – are less likely to have access to family and medical leave because they tend to work in smaller firms and to have more intermittent employment. Even when covered, the critics argue, working-class women can't afford to take unpaid leaves. Thus historian Alice Kessler-Harris worries that the Family and Medical Leave Act will benefit those who least need it – 'women and men who could in any event take the time off'. Legal scholar Martha Minow suggests more generally that the statute ignores not only social class but also a range of alternative family lifestyles. 'Problems of exclusion hobble the bill and expose it to charges of cultural, racial and class myopia'.[6]

These two charges center on the extent to which the FMLA seems to require denial of the special physiological and social character of motherhood, on the one hand, and of class and other group differences on the other.[7] The legislation is said to posit a single normative experience which is supposedly gender-neutral but actually male. The failure of the FMLA derives, in other words, from its assimilationist assumption that women can and should behave just like men – indeed, just like white, upper-middle-class men.

Feminists who make these charges often identify with the more progressive sectors of the contemporary women's movement. Their qualms about gender neutrality and assimilationism reflect their commitment to addressing the needs of working-class women, poor women and women of color. Looking longingly at European-style welfare programs, they belittle the ideological adequacy of the FMLA as much as they criticize its practical usefulness.

Equality, Gender Neutrality and Assimilationism

The feminist critique of the FMLA draws on more than a decade of political thought challenging traditional notions of equality.[8] This literature argues that our conventional understanding of equality is embedded in the Enlightenment construction of citizens as identical abstract individuals. The universal citizen turns out, however, not to be abstract. He is, in the first place, male, and he is also disembodied, strangely unencumbered by relationships or obligations, and, perhaps, of a dominant class and race. State policies that appear to be neutral thus in fact presume citizens to have gender (and class and race) specificity. Armed with these insights, scholars have unmasked the gendered character and group-specific workings of the modern welfare state. In this critique, difference is central while equality appears to be a scam devised to benefit men.

In the early 1980s, the challenge to equality became central to feminist efforts to address the needs of working mothers. A 1978

California statute mandating employers to provide pregnancy disability leave became the focus of litigation.[9] Mainstream feminist organizations opposed the statute because of its female specificity, but other feminists supported it as the best way to help working mothers. Given the special demands of pregnancy and motherhood on women workers, they asked, can treating women equally be fair? What about the family obligations for which women have disproportionate responsibility? Don't gender-neutral policies deny the unique character of women? Feminist scholars and activists divided in acrimonious debate. Confronted with the apparently unbridgeable opposition between equality and difference, many rejected equality and the gender-neutral policy framework of liberal feminism. Female specificity now seemed the policy approach most likely to accommodate the needs of women.

According to the FMLA's critics, in short, gender-neutral policies wear a mantle of fairness but actually disadvantage women by insisting they renounce special needs. That is, gender neutrality in policy is assumed to be unavoidably coupled with a conception of the just society as assimilationist. This assumption is not warranted, however. Although assimilationism was implicit in the efforts of most US feminist policy activists during the 1960s and 1970s, it is not the only possible position on the equality side of the equality-versus-difference dichotomy. A range of positions actually stretches across the distance between the dichotomy's poles, nearly all of which call for recognizing 'difference' (i.e. specificity) alongside equality.

At one end of the spectrum, assimilationism constructs women as fundamentally the same as men and supposes men to be the unencumbered abstract individuals of liberal theory. Targeting obstacles to women's full participation in society, assimilationists seek policies that treat women and men in an identical manner. Physiological sex differences are addressed by making a close analogy or equation of female-specific traits to already recognized characteristics. Assimilationists convert pregnancy, for example, into a temporary disability.

In the mid-1970s, androgyny, a less one-sided understanding of feminist objectives, became popular. Like assimilationism, androgyny uses analogy to deal with the stubborn specificity of sex-unique traits. But it shifts the object of the analogy from physiological characteristics to persons. That is, it invokes analogies not in order to convert sex-specific physical conditions to a supposedly universal basis, but to draw out the commonalities in the lives of differently sexed persons. In the case of pregnancy, androgyny constructs pregnant employees as different from their co-workers but with analogously special needs when temporarily unable to work. In this way it can acknowledge the special character of pregnancy within a formally gender-neutral legal framework. The 1978 Pregnancy Discrimination Act, for example, is a gender-neutral measure that implies androgyny, not assimilationism.[10] It does not define pregnancy as a temporary disability, but instead requires employers to make analogies across the bodily diversity of their employees – temporarily disabled or able-bodied, women or men.

A third vision of the meaning of equality has recently been proposed by political scientist Susan Moller Okin. In her view, which I call genderlessness, gender would be eliminated in the ideal future. As in assimilationism, a person's sex would become as irrelevant as eye color in shaping his or her social experience. But Okin recognizes, as assimilationists do not, that removing obstacles is not enough. To achieve the gender-free society requires a massive restructuring of social institutions and Okin proposes an array of practical measures: parental leave, subsidized day care, flexible working hours, more equitable post-divorce parenting arrangements and so on. In the long run, she argues, a genderless society will provide the best context for the development of human capacities and the realization of social justice.

Still on the equality side of the debate, I have suggested a fourth approach: differential consideration.[11] If we take differential consideration as our perspective, we envision a society in which individuals are diverse, embodied, and at times burdened with special needs and responsibilities, yet also deserving of equal treatment.

Each of these equality positions – assimilationism, androgyny, genderlessness and differential consideration – can be put into practice by means of gender-neutral measures. That is, no necessary association links gender neutrality as a legal form to assimilationism as a social vision. While some gender-neutral policies are indeed normatively male, others are gender-inclusive, even diversity-inclusive.[12] In other words, gender-neutral policies are not intrinsically unable to recognize human heterogeneity and connection. The trick, here, is in the specifics.

The Family and Medical Leave Act

The Family and Medical Leave Act of 1993 is a statute whose complex structure is not well understood. Feminist critics impugn its gender neutrality as imposing a male standard on women, but the media and popular opinion believe it to be a special-treatment policy to help working mothers care for their children. In reality, the FMLA is gender-neutral legislation that addresses a range of special needs in an inclusive manner. Because of widespread confusion about the statute, it is useful to review its provisions.

As its name suggests, the FMLA provides two distinct kinds of job- and benefit-protected leave. Family leave has drawn the most attention, for it represents an innovation in US employment policy. Family leave allows an employee time off to care for family members – a newborn, a newly adopted child, a seriously ill child, a spouse or a parent. Family leave will, of course, benefit women, who still bear primary responsibility for family caretaking. But family leave for men is not unimportant. Some will use it to be with a new baby or to accompany a sick child to the doctor. Others will take the leave to care for a mother with Alzheimer's or a father with a fractured hip.

Medical leave, the rarely mentioned other half of the FMLA, is not a new kind of benefit. Traditionally called disability leave, medical leave gives an employee time to recover from her or his own temporarily disabling health condition. Many workers will find the FMLA's medical leave component is at least as important to them as family leave. Only five US states and Puerto Rico require employers to allow a temporarily disabled employee to take time off. Until the passage of the FMLA, the majority of American workers had no job-protected disability leave. For a worker felled by medical emergency, job-guaranteed medical leave will be the FMLA's unexpected boon.

In sum, the FMLA provides benefits for a variety of off-the-job needs to women and men participating in a spectrum of household and family arrangements. Whether they need to care for others or for themselves, employees can take time off and then return to their jobs with seniority and health coverage intact. As for maternity leave, the legislation entitles a new mother to both medical leave (for difficulties in pregnancy and recovery from childbirth) and family leave (to care for the new baby). By dividing maternity leave in this way, public policy can now consider the special needs of working mothers without disregarding those of their co-workers.

Where is the FMLA positioned on the spectrum of equality positions described earlier? It is not an example of assimilationism, because it does not rigidly provide the same benefits for all. Nor is it an example of the androgyny approach, because it addresses differences directly, not by means of analogy. And it is also not within the genderlessness perspective, because its construction of special needs is affirmative. In my interpretation, the

133

FMLA is an example of legislation conceptualized in terms of differential consideration. It recognizes that employees all have personal needs and family responsibilities – and that their employers should acknowledge these needs. By addressing a diversity of special needs within a formally gender-neutral framework, the legislation assumes employees to be heterogeneous, embodied, encumbered, sometimes specially needy, but also equally entitled. That is, it posits a new sort of normative worker.

The Critique Revisited

The media, the public and many feminists do not appreciate the innovative design of the Family and Medical Leave Act. Relying on a set of familiar pairings, they interpret the statute in terms of dichotomies: equality / difference, same treatment / special treatment, gender neutrality / female specificity and so forth. Thus they miss the way the FMLA resists such oppositions by constructing the normative worker in a new way. And they make the charges that the measure cannot encompass women's special difference and that it is a class-biased or 'yuppie' bill.

As demonstrated in the previous section, the FMLA does not disregard the specialness of pregnancy and motherhood. The strength of differential consideration as a policy orientation is precisely its ability to affirm specificity without giving up universalism. Feminists designed the FMLA to address women's particular situation as mothers and simultaneously to offer benefits on an equal basis to all. Launched to help women workers, the statute turns out to have a broader scope. Indeed, I suspect that the general lack of job-guaranteed temporary disability leave in the US workplace will make medical leave for non-maternity purposes the most frequently used benefit in the FMLA's package.

The critics' inability to see the FMLA as a differential consideration policy in part flows from an underestimation of the range of available policy options. Believing they must choose between equality in the form of parental leave and difference in the form of maternity leave, they opt for difference.[13] But parental leave is only one – and not the best – of several possible gender-neutral policies that can address the needs of working mothers.

The rejection of the FMLA as class-biased legislation is problematic on several counts. It is of course true that the 40 per cent of the workforce not covered are those perhaps most in need of its benefits. But the statute's limited scope is a typical outcome of the difficult and conflict-ridden process of enacting reforms.[14]

Feminist academics who wish to do better for women too often assume it is possible to design legislation without considering context and history. Backing female-specific measures in emulation of European-style welfare provision, they overlook the peculiar trajectory of twentieth-century US social policy. In particular, where European female-specific policies have always been embedded in comprehensive welfare programs, the most powerful legacy of US female-specific legislation is discrimination. Recent reforms have eliminated the legal basis for most sex discrimination, but the tradition of paternalist yet discriminatory protection remains.

As the history of early twentieth-century protective legislation demonstrates, female-specific policies can all too easily be used to deny benefits to women. A more recent example is the female-specific design of the California statute that triggered litigation and the 1980s equality-versus-difference debates.[15] The statute covered women in small firms, with ambiguous consequences. It required employers to provide pregnancy disability leave, an important benefit, but it also allowed firms to exclude pregnancy from their health plans. Working-class women have a pressing need for both kinds of benefits, but I doubt they would choose access to *unpaid* disability leave over coverage of the medical costs of pregnancy.

Feminist critics of the FMLA also misread the legislation's value to those working-class women it covers. Here again, the baseline for comparison is not Europe but the US. Faced with a family crisis, American workers have traditionally had no protection. Thus the job- and benefit-guaranteed leave offered by the FMLA sets an important new labor standard. Painfully limited though the benefits are, they are significantly better than nothing. As Karen Nussbaum, then of the Service Employees International Union and now director of the Women's Bureau, put it in testimony to Congress: 'Though it is hard for a low-wage worker to take an unpaid leave, it is harder to lose your job entirely and start looking for a new one after the birth or illness of a child'.[16] The Family and Medical Leave Act begins to provide another option.

Conclusion

Whether female-specific or gender-neutral, US public policy is not likely soon to provide the benefits women workers need: income replacement while on leave, adequate health care, quality child care, better schools and housing, and so on. The American women's movement has been struggling for years simply to win a bit of unpaid leave for mothers. Employers continue to get away with not providing what little the law requires, particularly in small firms where working-class women often work. In the contemporary US context – a stingy welfare state, a tradition of discriminatory protection, divide-and-conquer management, propensity to backlash and persistent economic recession – female-specific measures remain risky.

With all its limitations, the Family and Medical Leave Act offers a significant new approach to social provision in the US workplace. Employers must henceforth acknowledge the off-the-job needs of their workers. And they must do so in a way that respects their employees' diversity – in gender, parenthood, family status, household structure, stage in the life cycle and so forth. The FMLA may also become the basis for an expansion of such specificity-affirming benefits. Even in the difficult economic climate of the late twentieth century, some state and local family and medical leave legislation already goes further – covering workers in smaller firms, providing longer leaves, and defining family membership and caretaking needs more broadly.[17] Paid leave may also be entering the policy agenda. Feminist policy analysts point, for example, to the effectiveness of mandatory temporary disability insurance (TDI) laws, which require even tiny firms to give paid leave to temporarily disabled employees.[18] Costs are spread widely by collecting small premiums from the state's many employers and/or employees. Why not use the same approach to fund paid family and medical leave for all workers?

The Family and Medical Leave Act shows that the alternative to female-specificity is not necessarily an uncaring yuppie-style assimilationism. Feminists can refuse to be pushed to one side of the supposed equality/difference dichotomy. And they can look more creatively for policies that embody the kind of radical approach to heterogeneity I am calling differential consideration.

NOTES

Chapter 1: Introduction

1. See, for example, Alice Echols, *Daring to Be Bad: Radical Feminism in America, 1967–1975* (Minneapolis: University of Minnesota Press, 1989); Sara Evans, *Personal Politics: The Roots of Women's Liberation in the Civil Rights Movement and the New Left* (New York: Alfred A. Knopf, 1979); Cynthia Harrison, *On Account of Sex: The Politics of Women's Issues, 1945–1968* (Berkeley: University of California Press, 1988); Myra Marx Ferree and Beth B. Hess, *Controversy and Coalition: The New Feminist Movement across Three Decades of Change*, rev. edn. (New York: Twayne Publishers, 1994). Although I am sympathetic to Ferree's and Hess's use of the term 'new feminist movement' to refer to the US women's movement of the past 35 years, I retain the more conventional, if imprecise, term 'second-wave feminism'.

2. For example, Robin Morgan, ed., *Sisterhood Is Powerful: An Anthology of Writings from the Women's Liberation Movement* (New York: Vintage Books, 1970); Deborah Babcox and Madeline Belkin, eds, *Liberation Now! Writings from the Women's Liberation Movement* (New York: Dell Publishing, 1971); Toni Cade, ed., *The Black Woman: An Anthology* (New York: New American Library, 1970); Vivian Gornick and Barbara K. Moran, eds, *Woman in Sexist Society: Studies in Power and Powerlessness* (New York: Basic Books, 1971); Gerda Lerner, ed., *Black Women in White America: A Documentary History* (New York: Pantheon Books, 1972); Miriam Schneir, ed., *Feminism: The Essential Historical Writings* (New York: Vintage Books, 1972).

3. See, for example, Frances M. Beal, 'Double Jeopardy: To Be Black and Female', in Morgan, *Sisterhood Is Powerful*, 340–53; Celestine Ware, *Woman Power: The Movement for Women's Liberation* (New York: Tower Publications, 1970), chap. 2; Cade, *The Black Woman*; Angela Davis, 'Reflections on the Black Woman's Role in the Community of Slaves', *Black Scholar* 3, no. 4 (December 1971), 3–15; Joyce Ladner, *Tomorrow's Tomorrow: The Black Woman* (New York: Doubleday, 1972); Pauli Murray, *Song in a Weary Throat* (New York: Harper and Row, 1987); Miriam Schneir, ed., *Feminism in Our Time: The Essential Writings, World War II to the Present* (New York:

Vintage Books, 1994), 171–87. On the race and class heterogeneity of the early years of second-wave feminism, see also Ferree and Hess, *Controversy and Coalition*, 92–9 and passim.

4. These two categories do not exhaust the range of perspectives within the women's liberation movement. In particular, they fail to capture the early activism of Black and lesbian women's liberationists. On socialist feminism, see also Chapter 3 below.

5. Even today, otherwise well-informed feminist commentators tend to discuss the women's movement in partial terms, as either a purely liberal enterprise or a wholly radical product of the late 1960s. For a rare effort to incorporate both stories into an integrated portrayal, see Ferree and Hess, *Controversy and Coalition*.

6. These practices and norms took a variety of race- and class-differentiated forms; Evelyn Nakano Glenn, 'From Servitude to Service Work: Historical Continuities in the Racial Division of Paid Reproductive Labor', *Signs* 18 (Autumn 1992), 1–43; Lise Vogel, 'U.S. Maternity Policy in Transition: From Protection and Denial to Equality', unpublished manuscript, 1993.

7. For a useful overview, see Teresa Amott, *Caught in the Crisis: Women and the U.S. Economy Today* (New York: Monthly Review Press, 1993).

8. Global restructuring is taking even more virulent forms in Eastern Europe and the Third World. Indeed, I speculate that the brutal series of invasions, armed conflagrations, civil wars and so-called ethnic cleansings sweeping the globe since the 1980s should be conceptualized as a new form of world war – which implies also that we recognize World War III to be already under way.

9. Conferences on socialism: Socialist Scholars (New York City), Rethinking Marxism (Amherst, MA). New journals: *Rethinking Marxism*; *Transformation: Marxist Boundary Work in Theory, Economics, Politics, and Culture*. Essay collections: Karen Hansen and Ilene Philipson, eds, *Women, Class, and the Feminist Imagination: A Socialist-Feminist Reader* (Philadelphia, PA: Temple University Press, 1990); Norma Stoltz Chinchilla and Martha E. Gimenez, eds, special issue on 'Marxist-Feminist Theory', *Gender & Society* 5 (1991), 286–407; Sonia Kruks, Rayna Rapp and Marilyn B. Young, eds, *Promissory Notes: Women in the Transition to Socialism* (New York: Monthly Review Press, 1989). Academic conference: Ninth Berkshire Conference on the History of Women, Vassar College, Poughkeepsie, NY, June 1993.

10. Tim Golden, 'Rebels Determined to Build Socialism in Mexico', *New York Times*, 4 January 1994, sec. A, p. 3. As it turns out, the aims of the Chiapas insurrection, the first postmodern guerrilla uprising, center not on socialism but on a 'new way of approaching the problem of power' in making a democratic transition to the new society. See 'The Second Declaration of the Lacandon' (11 June 1994), translated in the *Anderson Valley Advertiser* (Boonville, CA), 2

August 1994. Cf. John Ross, *Rebellion from the Roots: Indian Uprising in Chiapas* (Monroe, ME: Common Courage Press, 1995).

11. Evans, *Personal Politics*; Doug McAdam, *Freedom Summer* (New York: Oxford University Press, 1988).
12. Vivian Gornick, *The Romance of American Communism* (New York: Basic Books, 1977), 7.
13. Cf. Evelyn Fox Keller's description of graduate work as a woman in physics at Harvard, an experience not at all comparable to my own as an undergraduate in mathematics but one that I recognize; 'The Anomaly of a Woman in Physics', in *Working It Out: 23 Women Writers, Artists, Scientists, and Scholars Talk about Their Lives and Work*, ed. Sara Ruddick and Pamela Daniels (New York: Pantheon Books, 1977), 77–91. I am grateful to Barry Mazur for this reference.
14. That I could seem to flourish in art history while a woman like Fox Keller was driven from physics no doubt reflects the distinct traditions of the two fields. Fox Keller's observations about the departmental culture at Harvard strike me as reminiscent of my years there as well, as do the autobiographical portrayals of favored Harvard 'daughters' by Pamela Daniels, Sara Ruddick and, especially, Marilyn Young, in Ruddick and Daniels, *Working It Out*.
15. For the sit-ins, see William H. Chafe, *Civilities and Civil Rights: Greensboro, North Carolina, and the Black Struggle for Freedom* (New York: Oxford University Press, 1980). For the peace organization, Tocsin, see Todd Gitlin, *The Sixties: Years of Hope, Days of Rage* (New York: Bantam Books, 1987), 87–101. For SNCC, see Clayborne Carson, *In Struggle: SNCC and the Black Awakening of the 1960s* (Cambridge, MA: Harvard University Press, 1981); John Dittmer, *The Struggle for Civil Rights in Mississippi* (Urbana: University of Illinois Press, 1994). My use of the term 'Black' here is of course anachronistic; until the mid-1960s, the proper term was 'Negro'.
16. For the volunteers' experience in the Freedom Schools and voter registration campaigns, see McAdam, *Freedom Summer*; Sally Belfrage, *Freedom Summer* (New York: Viking Press, 1965); Elizabeth Sutherland, ed., *Letters from Mississippi* (New York: McGraw Hill, 1965); Mary Aickin Rothschild, *A Case of Black and White: Northern Volunteers and the Southern Freedom Summers, 1964–1965* (Westport CT: Greenwood Press, 1982).
17. For the first discussions of women's liberation, which took place among women in SNCC in the South and in SDS, see Echols, *Daring to Be Bad*; Evans, *Personal Politics*; and Schneir, *Feminism in Our Time*, 89–94, 103–24. For an account of the Boston women's liberation organization Bread and Roses, see Ann Popkin, 'The Personal Is Political: The Women's Liberation Movement', in *They Should Have Served That Cup of Coffee*, ed. Dick Cluster (Boston, MA: South End Press, 1979), 181–222, and idem, 'The Social Experience of Bread and Roses: Building a Community and Creating a

Culture', in Hansen and Philipson, *Women, Class, and the Feminist Imagination*, 182–212.

18. Lillian S. Robinson and Lise Vogel, 'Modernism and History', *New Literary History* 3 (1971), 177–99; Lise Vogel, 'Fine Arts and Feminism: The Awakening Consciousness', *Feminist Studies* 2 (1974), 3–37, reprinted in *Feminist Art Criticism: An Anthology*, ed. Arlene Raven, Cassandra L. Langer and Joanna Frueh (Ann Arbor, MI: UMI Research Press, 1988), 21–57. Reading such early 1970s criticism in 1992, Jane Gallop is surprised to find discussion of issues of race and class as well as gender – thus registering the extent to which the history of second-wave feminism has been revised; see her *Around 1981: Academic Feminist Literary Theory* (New York: Routledge, 1992), 78–80. For more on the rewriting of this history, see Chapter 8 below.

19. E.g. Lise Vogel, 'The Earthly Family', *Radical America*, 7, nos 4–5 (July–October 1973), 9–50; idem, *Women Workers: Some Basic Statistics* (Boston, MA: New England Free Press, 1971); idem, ' "Their Own Work": Two Documents from the Nineteenth-Century Labor Movement', *Signs* 1 (Spring 1976), 787–802; idem, ' "Humorous Incidents and Sound Common Sense": More on the New England Mill Women', *Labor History* 19 (1978), 280–6.

20. McAdam, *Freedom Summer*, 239.

21. James Baldwin, *The Fire Next Time* (New York: Delta Books, 1964), 116.

22. For the contemporary view that constructs antiracist work as 'an act of compassion for an "other", an optional, extra project, but not one intimately and organically linked to our own lives', see Ruth Frankenberg, *White Women, Race Matters: The Social Construction of Whiteness* (Minneapolis: University of Minnesota Press, 1993), 6. Frankenberg adds that 'racism can, in short, be conceived as something external to us rather than as a system that shapes our daily experiences and sense of self' (6). To well-meaning white feminists, 'the idea of being part of the problem of racism [is] genuinely shocking' (3). Evidently, each generation of activists must learn this lesson for itself.

23. Lillian Smith, *Killers of the Dream* (New York: W.W. Norton, 1949); W.J. Cash, *The Mind of the South* (New York: Alfred A. Knopf, 1941); John Dollard, *Caste and Class in a Southern Town*, 3rd edn. (New York: Anchor Books, 1957); Calvin C. Hernton, *Sex and Racism in America* (New York: Grove Press, 1965). With today's intellectual sophistication about race, class and gender, these texts seem weak, full of embarassing gaffes and worse. In my reading at the time, however, their limitations were far outweighed by the insights they offered.

24. Thomas Kuhn, *The Structure of Scientific Revolutions* (Chicago: University of Chicago Press, 1962).

25. Indeed, I am startled to see a family resemblance between my think-

ing as a feminist about equality and my first publication in art history, which suggested the existence in pre-Renaissance Europe of a way of seeing I named 'polyphonic'. The individual whose way of seeing was polyphonic 'may have both seen and created in terms of independent themes or systems ... each with its own identity and meaning' – for example, iconographic, ontological, temporal or formal. 'Thus there would have been a delight in and fluency with the possibilities of "polyphony".' With the Renaissance, a new kind of visual organization smoothed out the polyphonic narrative's celebration of independent voices. This displacement of visual polyphony represented, I implied, a loss. Lise Vogel, 'Flexibility Versus Formalism', *Art Journal* 27 (1968), 271–8.

Naive in its presentation, the article's proposal of a shift from a polyphonic seeing to one framed in terms of separable and symmetrical overlays still seems valid to me. In place of the rich multiplicity of voices in Roman and medieval narratives, the High Renaissance imposed a new kind of splitting of form from meaning together with bilateral symmetry as the dominant formal paradigm. Two decades later, I found myself resisting the imposition of dichotomous notions of equality and rejecting monolithic accounts of the history of feminism (see Chapters 8–10 below). Could it be that in both my older and more recent intellectual moves I was recalling the freedom struggle's vision of an heterogeneity-affirming justice?

26. Following local demographics, the Boston-based women's liberation movement of the late 1960s and early 1970s was, I believe, more white than that in other cities. It may also have been more student and middle-class. On diversity in second-wave feminism, see notes 2–3 above and the accompanying text.

27. Hazel V. Carby, 'The Multicultural Wars', *Radical History Review* 54 (1992), 7–18; Linda Gordon, 'On "Difference"', *Genders* 10 (1991), 91–111; Maria Lugones, 'Purity, Impurity, and Separation', *Signs* 19 (Winter 1994), 458–79; Sherene Razack, 'What Is to Be Gained by Looking White People in the Eye? Culture, Race, and Gender in Cases of Sexual Violence', *Signs* 19 (Summer 1994), 894–923.

Chapter 2: Questions on the Woman Question

1. In 'Questions on the Woman Question' I named the two positions the 'family argument' and the 'social production argument'. In *Marxism and the Oppression of Women* I revised the terminology, opposing the 'dual-systems perspective' to the 'social reproduction perspective'. For more on the social reproduction approach, see Chapter 6 below, a reply to a critique of 'Questions on the Woman Question'.

2. While socialism and Marxism are of course not synonymous, I use the terms socialist feminism and Marxist feminism interchangeably, following ordinary practice within the contemporary women's movement. Socialist feminism is not, moreover, the exclusive province of women:

the New American Movement, for example, calls itself a socialist feminist organization.

3. Juliet Mitchell, 'Women: The Longest Revolution', *New Left Review* no. 40 (November–December 1966), 11–37; Eli Zaretsky, 'Capitalism, the Family, and Personal Life', *Socialist Revolution* nos 13–14 (January–April 1973), 69–125, and no. 15 (May–June 1973), 19–70; Heidi Hartmann and Amy Bridges, 'The Unhappy Marriage of Marxism and Feminism: Towards a More Progressive Union', *Capital and Class*, no. 8 (Summer 1979), 1–33.

4. These few remarks barely summarize what in fact is an extremely complex situation. Socialist feminism is not a monolithic trend and it offers much that is valuable and attractive. Most important, many have turned to socialist feminism in the absence of a sufficiently developed theoretical and practical commitment to women's liberation within the rest of the left.

5. This formulation, usually attributed to François-Charles Fourier, is actually a significantly altered paraphrase of his remarks in *Theorie des quatre mouvements* (Paris: Pauvert, 1967), 147. See Karl Marx and Frederick Engels, *The Holy Family* (Moscow: Progress Publishers, 1975), 230.

6. August Bebel, *Woman under Socialism* (New York: Schocken Books, 1970), 1, 4.

7. Ibid., 5, 115.

8. V.I. Lenin, *The Emancipation of Women* (New York: International Publishers, 1966), 97.

9. Nancy Smith Barrett of the Urban Institute estimates that fewer than 16 per cent of US households in 1976 consisted of a working husband, a wife not in the labor force, and one or more children under the age of 18; 'Data Needs for Evaluating the Labor Market Status of Women', unpublished paper, 1978. The Department of Labor observes that 'the notion persists that the "average" family is made up of a husband, a nonworking wife, and two children. In actuality, this type of four-person family accounts for only seven percent of all husband–wife families'; *Employment in Perspective: Working Women*, Bureau of Labor Statistics, Report 531, April 1978. For married women's participation in the labor force, see Howard Hayghe, 'Families and the Rise of Working Wives – An Overview', *Monthly Labor Review* 99, no. 5 (May 1976).

10. Karl Marx, *Capital* (Moscow: Progress Publishers, n.d.), vol. 1:460.

11. Frederick Engels, *The Origin of the Family, Private Property and the State* (New York: International Publishers, 1972), 137–8.

12. For example, Albert Szymanski, 'Trends in the American Working Class', *Socialist Revolution* no. 10 (July–August 1972); and Charles Anderson, *The Political Economy of Social Class* (Englewood Cliffs, NJ: Prentice-Hall, 1974).

13. For example, Nicos Poulantzas, *Classes in Contemporary Capitalism* (London: New Left Books, 1975).

14. The same comments hold for the frequent identification by Marxists of 'workers' with 'the working class'.
15. Engels, *Origin*, 221.
16. Lenin, *Emancipation*, 15–16.
17. Ibid., 83 and passim.
18. Bebel, *Woman*, 5–6.
19. Lenin, *Emancipation*, 80.
20. Engels, *Origin*, 137; cf. Lenin, *Emancipation*, 43. Engels and Lenin argued that democratic rights within a capitalist society enable all – women, workers, oppressed nationalities – to participate in the class struggle on the strongest possible terms. But they did not address the problem of the theoretical specificity of sex as opposed to race oppression. At the economic level, the obvious place to look for this specificity is in the area of unpaid household labor, an activity associated with divisions of labor according to sex but not with divisions according to race or nationality. Yet the near invisibility of this domestic labor within Marxist theory, at least until recently, has blocked any attempts in this direction. Curiously ignoring the enormous quantity of labor devoted to housework, Marxist theorists have treated women's situation as a question of democratic rights and ideological oppression. Unless the theoretical distinction between sex and race oppression is clarified, the danger persists of first paralleling and then ranking them – and of thus falling into an unscientific and moralistic conception of the fight for democratic rights. Cf. Lise Vogel, 'On: "Class Roots of Feminism" ', *Monthly Review* 28, no. 9 (February 1977), 52–60 (reworked in Chapter 7 in the present volume).
21. Engels, *Origin*, 71.
22. For a preliminary discussion of variant family forms in these terms, see Lise Vogel, 'The Contested Domain: A Note on the Family in the Transition to Capitalism', *Marxist Perspectives* 1, no. 1 (Spring 1978), 50–73.
23. Lenin, *Emancipation*, 83–4.

Chapter 4: Marxism and Feminism: Unhappy Marriage, Trial Separation or Something Else?

1. Heidi Hartmann, 'The Unhappy Marriage of Marxism and Feminism: Toward a More Progressive Union', in *Women and Revolution: A Discussion of the Unhappy Marriage of Marxism and Feminism*, ed. Lydia Sargent (Boston, MA: South End Press, 1981), 1–41.
2. Ibid., 32.
3. Ibid., 2. The first version of the essay circulated without a subtitle; Heidi Hartmann and Amy Bridges, 'The Unhappy Marriage of Marxism and Feminism', working draft, July 1975.
4. Rosalind Petchesky, 'Dissolving the Hyphen: Report on Marxist-Feminist Groups 1–5', in *Capitalist Patriarchy and the Case for*

Socialist Feminism, ed. Zillah Eisenstein (New York: Monthly Review Press, 1979). Joan Kelly, 'The Doubled Vision of Feminist Theory', *Feminist Studies* 5 (1979), 216–27.
5. Hartmann, 'Unhappy Marriage', 31.
6. Juliet Mitchell, 'Women: The Longest Revolution', *New Left Review* no. 40 (November–December 1966) 11–37; idem, *Woman's Estate* (Baltimore, MD: Penguin Books, 1971).
7. Mitchell, 'Women', 15, 16.
8. Ibid., 35; idem, *Woman's Estate*, 150.
9. Mitchell, 'Women', 34
10. Ibid.
11. Murdock argued that the universal nuclear family incorporates the 'four functions fundamental to human social life – the sexual, the economic, the reproductive, and the educational [i.e. that pertaining to socialization]'. George Murdock, *Social Structure* (New York: Macmillan, 1949), 10.
12. Mitchell, *Woman's Estate*, 86.
13. Margaret Benston, 'The Political Economy of Women's Liberation', *Monthly Review* 21, no. 4 (September 1969), 13–27; Peggy Morton, 'A Woman's Work Is Never Done', in *From Feminism to Liberation*, ed. Edith Altbach (Cambridge, MA: Schenkman Publishing, 1971), 211–27.
14. Benston, 'Political Economy', 16, 20, 22.
15. Morton, 'Woman's Work', 214, 215–16.
16. For early critiques of Benston, see Morton, 'Woman's Work'; Mickey and John Rowntree, 'Notes on the Political Economy of Women's Liberation', *Monthly Review* 21, no. 7 (December 1969), 26–32; Roberta Salper, 'The Development of the American Women's Liberation Movement, 1967–1971', in *Female Liberation*, ed. Roberta Salper (New York: Alfred A. Knopf, 1972), 169–84.
17. Mariarosa Dalla Costa, 'Women and the Subversion of the Community', in *The Power of Women and the Subversion of the Community* (Bristol: Falling Wall Press, 1972), 19–54.
18. Ibid., 19.
19. Ibid., 52, n. 12; 39.
20. Ibid., 34, 47.
21. Paul Smith, 'Domestic Labour and Marx's Theory of Value', in *Feminism and Materialism: Women and Modes of Production*, ed. Annette Kuhn and Annemarie Wolpe (Boston, MA: Routledge and Kegan Paul, 1978), 198–219; Ira Gerstein, 'Domestic Work and Capitalism', *Radical America* 7, nos 4–5 (July–October 1973), 101–28; Maxine Molyneux, 'Beyond the Domestic Labour Debate', *New Left Review* 116 (July–August 1979), 3–27.
22. Mitchell, *Woman's Estate*, 99.
23. Shulamith Firestone, *The Dialectic of Sex: The Case for Feminist Revolution* (New York: William Morrow, 1970), 12; Kate Millett, *Sexual Politics* (New York: Doubleday, 1970).

24. Eisenstein, *Capitalist Patriarchy*, 6. For Mitchell's critique of radical feminism, see her *Woman's Estate*, 82–96.
25. Sheila Rowbotham, *Man's World, Woman's Consciousness* (Baltimore, MD: Penguin Books, 1973), 117. Early and influential discussions of patriarchy include Hartmann and Bridges, 'Unhappy Marriage'; Joan Kelly-Gadol, 'The Social Relation of the Sexes: Methodological Implications of Women's History', *Signs* 1 (Summer 1976), 809–23; Gayle Rubin, 'The Traffic in Women: Notes on the "Political Economy" of Sex', in *Toward an Anthropology of Women*, ed. Rayna R. Reiter (New York: Monthly Review Press, 1975), 157–210.
26. Mitchell used the concept of a mode of reproduction as early as 1966; 'Women', 21. For other examples, see Renate Bridenthal, 'The Dialectics of Production and Reproduction in History', *Radical America* 10, no. 2 (March–April 1976), 3–11; Jean Gardiner, 'The Political Economy of Domestic Labour in Capitalist Society', in *Dependence and Exploitation in Work and Marriage*, ed. Diana Leonard Barker and Sheila Allen (New York: Longman, 1976), 109–20; Bridget O'Laughlin, 'Marxist Approaches in Anthropology', *Annual Review of Anthropology* 4 (1975), 341–70, esp. 365–6.
27. Veronica Beechey, 'On Patriarchy', *Feminist Review* 3 (1979), 66–82; Val Burris, 'The Dialectic of Women's Oppression: Notes on the Relation between Capitalism and Patriarchy', *Berkeley Journal of Sociology* 27 (1982), 51–74; Roisin McDonough and Rachel Harrison, 'Patriarchy and Relations of Production', in Kuhn and Wolpe, *Feminism and Materialism*, 153–72; Felicity Edholm, Olivia Harris and Kate Young, 'Conceptualising Women', *Critique of Anthropology* nos 9–10 (1977), 101–30.
28. Iris Young, 'Socialist Feminism and the Limits of Dual Systems Theory', *Socialist Review* nos 50–1 (March–June 1980): 169–88; Beechey, 'On Patriarchy'.
29. See, for example, the following collections: 'Women's Issue', *Critique of Anthropology* 9–10 (1977); Eisenstein, *Capitalist Patriarchy*; Kuhn and Wolpe, *Feminism and Materialism*; Sargent, *Women and Revolution*. See also the works cited above in notes 27 and 28.

Chapter 5: Engels's *Origin*: A Defective Formulation

1. Frederick Engels, *The Origin of the Family, Private Property and the State* (New York: International Publishers, 1972), 71.
2. Engels to Kautsky, 16 February and 26 April, 1884, in Karl Marx and Frederick Engels, *Selected Correspondence*, 2nd edn. (Moscow: Progress Publishers, 1965), 368, 372. See also Lawrence Krader, ed. *The Ethnological Notebooks of Karl Marx* (Assen: Van Gorcum, 1972), 388–90.
3. For Bebel's work, see Lise Vogel, *Marxism and the Oppression of Women: Toward a Unitary Theory* (New Brunswick, NJ: Rutgers University Press, 1983), 96–103.

4. Lewis Morgan, *Ancient Society* (New York: Holt, 1877); Krader, *Ethnological Notebooks*.
5. Morgan, *Ancient Society*, 561–2.
6. See, for example, the introduction by Eleanor Leacock in Lewis Morgan, *Ancient Society* (Cleveland, OH: World Publishing Co., 1963).
7. Morgan, *Ancient Society*, vii, 3, 8.
8. Ibid., vii.
9. Krader, *Ethnological Notebooks*, 11, and 365, n. 21. See also U. Santamaria, 'Review Article: The Ethnological Notebooks of Karl Marx, ed. by L. Krader', *Critique of Anthropology* nos 4–5 (Autumn 1975), 156–64.
10. Engels, *Origin*, 93.
11. Ibid., 101–10.
12. Ibid., 117.
13. Ibid., 119–20.
14. Ibid., 120–1.
15. Ibid., 128.
16. Ibid., 128, 129.
17. Ibid., 132, 135.
18. Ibid., 135–8.
19. Ibid., 137.
20. Ibid. Cf. Karl Marx, *Capital*, vol. 1 (Moscow: Progress Publishers, n.d.), 460.
21. Engels, *Origin*, 138–46.
22. Ibid., 139.
23. Ibid., 171.
24. Marx to J.D. Schweitzer, 24 January 1865, in Marx and Engels, *Selected Correspondence*, 153.
25. Engels, *Origin*, 218–25.
26. Ibid., 223, 224, 235; see also 119, 161.
27. Ibid., 71–2.
28. Karl Marx and Friedrich Engels, *Werke* (Berlin: Dietz Verlag, 1956–), vol. 36: 33–4; see also 39, 41 and 54, and Engels, *Origin*, 129. On the textual similarity, see also H. Kent Geiger, *The Family in Soviet Russia* (Cambridge, MA: Harvard University Press, 1968), 30–2.
29. Karl Marx and Frederick Engels, *Collected Works* (New York: International Publishers, 1975–), vol. 5: 43.
30. Marx and Engels, *Collected Works*, vol. 5: 33, 46; Engels, *Origin*, 121, 134, 137.
31. Marx and Engels, *Collected Works*, vol. 5: 46; Engels, *Origin*, 121–2, 129, 131, 137.
32. On the turn-of-the-century socialists, see Geiger, *Family in Soviet Russia*, 31–2; similar opinions are expressed in Barry Hindess and Paul Hirst, *Pre-Capitalist Modes of Production* (London: Routledge and Kegan Paul, 1975), 58–9. On the Soviet view, see Bernhard

Stern, 'Engels on the Family', *Science & Society* 12 (1948), 42–64, esp. 48, n. 10.
33. Engels, *Origin*, 71.

Chapter 6: From the Woman Question to Women's Liberation

1. Johanna Brenner and Nancy Holmstrom, 'Women's Self-Organization: Theory and Strategy', *Monthly Review* 34, no. 11 (April 1983) 34–46; my reply follows on pp. 47–52. The version of the reply I publish here is substantially revised, drawing in particular on my comment in *Contemporary Sociology* 13 (1984), 601, and on 'Domestic Labor Revisited and Other Puzzles', a paper presented at the 1994 Conference of Socialist Economists, held in Leeds, England.
2. My understanding of theory as skeletal in nature to some extent converges with Iris Young's discussion of a 'pragmatic theorizing [that] is not concerned to give an account of a whole'; Iris Marion Young, 'Gender as Seriality: Thinking about Women as a Social Collective', *Signs* 18 (Spring 1994), 713–38, esp. 718. In terms of Young's concept of gender as seriality, my project here has been to identify aspects of the way women are serialized by the processes of capitalist social reproduction.
3. For the discussion in this and the following paragraphs, see also Lise Vogel, *Marxism and the Oppression of Women: Toward a Unitary Theory* (New Brunswick, NJ: Rutgers University Press, 1983), chaps 10, 11.
4. Ibid., 151–6.
5. V.I. Lenin, *The Emancipation of Women* (New York: International Publishers, 1966), 80.
6. For example, Meredith Tax, *The Rising of the Women: Feminist Solidarity and Class Conflict, 1880–1917* (New York: Monthly Review Press, 1980); Kumari Jayawardena, *Feminism and Nationalism in the Third World* (London: Zed Books, 1986); Sonia Kruks, Rayna Rapp and Marilyn B. Young, eds, *Promissory Notes: Women in the Transition to Socialism* (New York: Monthly Review Press, 1989).
7. I provide some illustrations drawn from specific historical examples in *Marxism and the Oppression of Women*.
8. Gail Omvedt, 'Women's Liberation Conference Held in India', *Guardian*, 10 December 1980; Crystal Eastman, 'Feminism', in *On Woman and Revolution*, ed. Blanche Wiesen Cook (New York: Oxford University Press, 1978), 51.

Chapter 7: Class and Other Roots

1. See, for example, the work of Gloria Anzaldúa, Elsa Barkley Brown, Karen Fields, Maria Lugones and Patricia Williams, among others.

2. I use the plural 'movements' to stress the variety and discontinuity of what Sacks tends to treat monolithically.
3. Louis Althusser, 'Reply to John Lewis (Self Criticism)', *Marxism Today* (November 1972), 344.
4. At least four groupings of articles can be cited. First, the theoretically sophisticated articles published in England in *New Left Review* and the *Bulletin of the Conference of Socialist Economists*. Second, a number of American pieces written from a 'radical sociology' viewpoint in *Socialist Revolution* and *Insurgent Sociologist*. Third, the articles and pamphlets associated with the European wages for housework campaign. Fourth, work produced from within the socialist-feminist trend of the North American women's liberation movement. Virtually none of the authors in one grouping makes any mention, much less critique, of the work in the others. This is especially unfortunate where the subjects treated are the same, as in the various attempts to develop a Marxist analysis of housework using the categories of productive and unproductive labor. Surely it is time that we take ourselves and the task sufficiently seriously to build on each other's work.

Chapter 8: Telling Tales: Historians of Our Own Lives

1. Jane Gallop comments in 1989, for example, that 'race only posed itself as an urgent issue to me in the last couple of years'; *Conflicts in Feminism*, ed. Marianne Hirsch and Evelyn Fox Keller (New York: Routledge, 1990), 363. Nancy K. Miller suggests 1985 as the starting point for the feminist obligation to acknowledge 'race, class, ethnicity, geography, sexuality, as modes of being in the world that inflect a gendered identity'; *Getting Personal: Feminist Occasions and Other Autobiographical Acts* (New York: Routledge, 1991), 125.
2. For a description of how one such confrontation felt to a white participant, see Hirsch and Keller, *Conflicts in Feminism*, 382–4. Audre Lorde tells the story from the other side in *Sister Outsider: Essays and Speeches* (Trumansburg, NY: Crossing Press, 1984), 124–33 and passim.
3. Key moments in the process can be glimpsed in Ellen DuBois, Mari Jo Buhle, Temma Kaplan, Gerda Lerner and Carroll Smith-Rosenberg, 'Politics and Culture in Women's History: A Symposium', *Feminist Studies* 6 (1980), 26–64; Judith Kegan Gardiner, Elly Bulkin, Rena Grasso Patterson and Annette Kolodny, 'An Interchange on Feminist Criticism: On "Dancing through the Minefield" ', *Feminist Studies* 8 (1982), 629–75; Jane Marcus, 'Storming the Toolshed', *Signs* 7 (Spring 1982), 622–40.
4. Elsa Barkley Brown, ' "What Has Happened Here": The Politics of Difference in Women's History and Feminist Politics', *Feminist Studies* 18 (1992), 297. For 'gumbo ya ya', see Luisah Teish, *Jambalaya: The Natural Woman's Book of Personal Charms and Practical Rituals* (San Francisco, CA: Harper and Row, 1985), 139–67.

5. Miller, *Getting Personal*, xii; xvii, n. 6.
6. Cf. Lise Vogel, 'Flexibility versus Formalism', *Art Journal* 27 (1968), 271–8.
7. Nancy Hewitt, *Multiple Truths: The Personal, the Political, and the Postmodernist in Contemporary Feminist Scholarship*, working paper (Memphis, TN: Memphis State University Center for Research on Women, 1992).
8. The papers were subsequently published as Louise Newman, 'Critical Theory and the History of Women: What's at Stake in Deconstructing Women's History', *Journal of Women's History* 2 (1991), 58–68; and Joan Williams, 'Domesticity as the Dangerous Supplement of Liberalism', *Journal of Women's History* 2 (1991), 69–88.
9. Newman is more explicit in her adoption of this version of the history of women's history, but it is implicit in Williams's paper as well.
10. Joan Wallach Scott, *Gender and the Politics of History* (New York: Columbia University Press, 1988), 7.
11. Linda Gordon describes the study group in *Visions of History*, eds. Henry Abelove, Betsy Blackmar, Peter Dimock and Jonathan Schneer (New York: Pantheon Books, 1984), 76.
12. For the relationship between the emerging feminist scholarship of the early 1970s and the women's movement, see Ellen Carol DuBois, Gail Paradise Kelly, Elizabeth Lapovsky Kennedy, Carolyn W. Korsmeyer and Lillian S. Robinson, *Feminist Scholarship: Kindling in the Groves of Academe* (Urbana: University of Illinois Press, 1985); and Marilyn J. Boxer, 'For and about Women: The Theory and Practice of Women's Studies in the United States', *Signs* 7 (Spring 1982), 661–95.
13. Alice Echols captures some of the period's turbulence in *Daring to Be Bad: Radical Feminism in America, 1967–1975* (Minneapolis: University of Minnesota Press, 1989); see also Sara Evans, *Personal Politics: The Roots of Women's Liberation in the Civil Rights Movement and the New Left* (New York: Alfred A. Knopf, 1979). Echols's ground-breaking study, which chronicles the evolution of radical feminism by looking at its ideology and leading figures, should be followed by focused examination of other aspects of second-wave feminism. No new research is necessary, however, to document the fact that the slogan 'the personal is political' came from the radical women's liberation movement, and not from the suburban housewives whose plight was memorialized by Betty Friedan. I am therefore puzzled by Newman's claim that 'the discourse produced by the women's movement of the 1960s, as summarized by its slogan "the personal is political", was powerful and significant because it enabled specific groups of women, primarily white, middle-class suburban women, to reconceptualize their past experiences in new ways'. (Newman, 'Critical Theory', 63.) The notion that the women's movement of the late 1960s and early 1970s was a unified move-

ment of white middle-class women is widespread, appearing in scholarly as well as media and popular accounts.

14. Robin Morgan, ed., *Sisterhood Is Powerful: An Anthology of Writings from the Women's Liberation Movement* (New York: Vintage Books, 1970). Note that the articles cited did not have to stand alone to 'cover' their respective categories; for each group (e.g. Blacks, lesbians, Chicanas, youth), Morgan included a number of pieces, explaining in the Introduction that 'it was important to have more than one or two voices speak for so many sisters, and in differing ways' (xxvi).

15. Examples include: Deborah Babcox and Madeline Belkin, eds, *Liberation Now! Writings from the Women's Liberation Movement* (New York: Dell Publishing, 1971); Toni Cade, ed., *The Black Woman: An Anthology* (New York: New American Library, 1970); Nancy F. Cott, ed., *Root of Bitterness: Documents of the Social History of American Women* (New York: E. P. Dutton, 1972); Vivian Gornick and Barbara K. Moran, eds, *Woman in Sexist Society: Studies in Power and Powerlessness* (New York: Basic Books, 1971); Gerda Lerner, ed., *Black Women in White America: A Documentary History* (New York: Pantheon Books, 1972); Roberta Salper, ed., *Female Liberation: History and Current Politics* (New York: Alfred A. Knopf, 1972); Miriam Schneir, ed., *Feminism: The Essential Historical Writings* (New York: Vintage Books, 1972); Leslie B. Tanner, ed., *Voices from Women's Liberation* (New York: New American Library, 1970). Many of the essays in *Liberation Now!* were reprinted from *Up from Under*, a feminist journal published in New York City by white working-class women.

16. Berenice A. Carroll, ed., *Liberating Women's History: Theoretical and Critical Essays* (Urbana: University of Illinois Press, 1976); Milton Cantor and Bruce Laurie, eds, *Class, Sex, and the Woman Worker* (Westport, CT: Greenwood Press, 1977); Rosalyn Baxandall, Linda Gordon and Susan Reverby, eds, *America's Working Women* (New York: Vintage Books, 1976). For quick processing of my request for photocopies of the 1973 and 1974 Berkshire Conference programs, I am indebted to Susan J. von Salis of the Schlesinger Library on the History of Women in America at Radcliffe College.

17. For compelling discussions of this persistent failing on the part of even those with the best of intentions, see, among others, Audre Lorde, 'The Uses of Anger: Women Responding to Racism', in Lorde, *Sister Outsider*, 124–33; Margaret A. Simons, 'Racism and Feminism: A Schism in the Sisterhood', *Feminist Studies* 5 (1979), 384–401. See also Elizabeth V. Spelman, *Inessential Woman: Problems of Exclusion in Feminist Thought* (Boston, MA: Beacon Press, 1988).

18. Carroll Smith-Rosenberg, 'The New Woman and the New History', *Feminist Studies* 3 (1975), 185–98, esp. 186, 188; this article provides a useful description of the evolution from the 'traditional' women's history practiced in the 1960s to the 'new women's history' of the 1970s.

19. Joan Jacobs Brumberg and Nancy Tomes, 'Women in the Professions: A Research Agenda for American Historians', *Reviews in American History* 10 (1982), 275–96.
20. Nancy A. Hewitt, 'Beyond the Search for Sisterhood: American Women's History in the 1980s', *Social History* 10 (1985), 299–322; Linda K. Kerber, 'Separate Spheres, Female Worlds, Woman's Place: The Rhetoric of Women's History', *Journal of American History* 75 (1988), 9–39; Carroll Smith-Rosenberg, 'The Female World of Love and Ritual: Relations between Women in Nineteenth-Century America', *Signs* 1 (Autumn 1975), 1–30.
21. Echols, *Daring to Be Bad*, 6.
22. As a graduate student in art history in the 1960s, I was also influenced by the work of Thomas Kuhn, Rudolf Arnheim and Ernst Gombrich, all of whom deeply problematized the nature of knowledge and representation.
23. Newman, 'Critical Theory', 66.
24. DuBois et al., 'Politics and Culture'.
25. Ibid., 29, 34, 44, 47.
26. Ibid., 55, 63, 62.
27. For bibliography, see DuBois et al., *Feminist Scholarship*; see also the bibliographical survey in Lise Vogel, 'Feminist Scholarship: The Impact of Marxism', in *The Left Academy: Marxist Scholarship on American Campuses*, vol. 3, eds Bertell Ollman and Edward Vernoff (New York: Praeger Books, 1986), 1–34.
28. Kerber, 'Separate Spheres', 11.
29. Gerda Lerner, 'The Lady and the Mill Girl: Changes in the Status of Women in the Age of Jackson', *American Studies* 10 (1969), 5–15; Barbara Welter, 'The Cult of True Womanhood, 1820–1860', *American Quarterly* 18 (1966), 151–74. In her 1975 literature review, 'The New Woman', Smith-Rosenberg situates Lerner's article as 'pathbreaking', reflecting a dramatic shift to new questions; she places Welter's earlier piece in the 'transitional' category.
30. For discussion of analogous astonishment in the field of feminist law, analyzing it as based on generational succession and with an attempt to reach across the divide, see Wendy W. Williams, 'Notes from a First Generation', *University of Chicago Legal Forum* 1989 (1989), 99–113.
31. On the politics of difference, see, for example, Iris M. Young, 'Difference and Policy: Some Reflections in the Context of New Social Movements', *University of Cincinnati Law Review* 56 (1987), 535–50; and Hazel V. Carby, 'The Politics of Difference', *Ms Magazine*, September–October 1990, 84–5.
32. In preparing this paper, first as a conference commentary and then for publication, I have benefited from excellent advice as well as warm support from a number of colleagues. I am most grateful to Susan Reverby and Kathleen Daly, with whom I have had the pleasure of discussing these remarks thoroughly; their generous contribu-

tions of time, ideas and meticulous comments on multiple versions is a model of what collegial sisterhood can be. I want also to thank Eileen Boris for encouragement and references, Hester Eisenstein and Molly Nolan for thoughtful critiques at very short notice, and the audience at the Berkshire Conference for its enthusiastic reception of the entire panel.

Chapter 9: Beyond Equality: Some Feminist Questions

1. Lise Vogel, *Marxism and the Oppression of Women: Toward a Unitary Theory* (New Brunswick, NJ: Rutgers University Press, 1983), 89–90, 109–11, 118–22.
2. Robert W. Gordon, 'New Developments in Legal Theory', in *The Politics of Law: A Progressive Critique*, ed. David Kairys (New York: Pantheon Books, 1990), 413–25; Martha Minow, *Making All the Difference: Inclusion, Exclusion, and American Law* (Ithaca, NY: Cornell University Press, 1990), 164–72; Mark Tushnet, 'Critical Legal Studies: An Introduction to Its Origins and Underpinnings', *Journal of Legal Education* 36 (1986), 505–17.
3. For pioneering critiques, see Martha L. Fineman, 'Implementing Equality: Ideology, Contradiction and Social Change – A Study of Rhetoric and Results in the Regulation of the Consequences of Divorce', *Wisconsin Law Review* 1983 (1983), 789–886; Catharine A. MacKinnon, *Sexual Harassment of Working Women* (New Haven, CT: Yale University Press, 1979); Elizabeth Wolgast, *Equality and the Rights of Women* (Ithaca, NY: Cornell University Press, 1980); and the literature cited in n. 5, below. For overviews, see Deborah L. Rhode, *Justice and Gender: Sex Discrimination and the Law* (Cambridge, MA: Harvard University Press, 1989), 111–31, 305–21; Adelaide H. Villmoare, 'Women, Differences, and Rights as Practices: An Interpretive Essay and a Proposal', *Law and Society Review* 25 (1991), 385–410.
4. Sally J. Kenney, *For Whose Protection? Reproductive Hazards and Exclusionary Policies in the United States and Britain* (Ann Arbor: University of Michigan Press, 1992); Cynthia R. Daniels, *At Women's Expense: State Power and the Politics of Fetal Rights* (Cambridge, MA: Harvard University Press, 1993).
5. For early attempts to disentangle various positions within the poles of the debate, see Ann C. Scales, 'Towards a Feminist Jurisprudence', *Indiana Law Review* 56 (1980–1), 375–444; Sylvia Law, 'Rethinking Sex and the Constitution', *University of Pennsylvania Law Review* 132 (1984), 955–1040; Herma Hill Kay, 'Models of Equality', *University of Illinois Law Review* 1985 (1985), 39–88. Political philosophers and social scientists likewise discuss a range of positions covered by the notion of equality; early discussions include Alice S. Rossi, 'Sex Equality: The Beginning of Ideology', *Humanist*

29 (September–October 1969), 3–6+; Jean Bethke Elshtain, 'The Feminist Movement and the Question of Equality', *Polity* 7 (1975), 452–77; Mary C. Segers, 'Equality, Public Policy and Relevant Sex Differences', *Polity* 11 (1979), 319–39.

6. Christine A. Littleton, 'Reconstructing Sexual Equality', *California Law Review* 75 (1987), 1279–337.
7. I am indebted to Eloise Buker for suggesting that I make this distinction explicit. The 1993 Family and Medical Leave Act is an example of a formally gender-neutral measure that is inclusive in impact; see Chapter 10 below.
8. I propose a fourth symmetrist position, which I call 'differential consideration', in *Mothers on the Job: Maternity Policy in the U.S. Workplace* (New Brunswick, NJ: Rutgers University Press, 1993).
9. More precisely, assimilationism assumes as the norm male experience that is unencumbered by special problems or obligations inside or outside the workplace.
10. Wendy W. Williams, 'Equality's Riddle: Pregnancy and the Equal Treatment/Special Treatment Debate', *New York University Review of Law and Social Change* 13 (1984–5), 325–80, esp. 368, 363. See also ibid., 367, 369, and Nadine Taub and Wendy W. Williams, 'Will Equality Require More Than Assimilation, Accommodation or Separation from the Existing Social Structure?', *Rutgers Law Review* 37 (1985), 825–44, esp. 836, 838. Littleton uses the example of the adjustable lecture podium to illustrate her claim that restructuring flows only from the equality-as-acceptance approach; 'Reconstructing Sexual Equality', 1314.
11. Taub and Williams, 'Will Equality Require More', 838.
12. Susan Moller Okin, *Justice, Gender, and the Family* (New York: Basic Books, 1989), 171, 180, 184.
13. Most policy activists and mainstream feminist organizations continue to support the symmetrist strategies developed in the 1960s and 1970s.
14. Lucinda M. Finley, 'Transcending Equality Theory: A Way out of the Maternity and the Workplace Debate', *Columbia Law Review* 86 (1986), 1118–82, esp. 1143. Some asymmetrists discuss several variants of the equal-treatment perspective, all of which are said to come down to the same disadvantaging demand that women conform to standards developed for men. See, for example, Littleton, 'Reconstructing Sexual Equality', 1291–5.
15. Wolgast, *Equality and the Rights of Women*, 14, 42, 129.
16. Scales, 'Towards a Feminist Jurisprudence', 433.
17. Scales calls the special rights position 'bivalence', but this is probably a misapplication of Wolgast's use of the term in *Equality and the Rights of Women*, 16.
18. Catharine A. MacKinnon, *Feminism Unmodified: Discourses on Life and Law* (Cambridge, MA: Harvard University Press, 1987), 40.
19. Isabel Marcus and Paul J. Spiegelman, eds, 'Feminist Discourse,

Moral Values, and the Law – a Conversation,' *Buffalo Law Review* 34 (1985), 11–87, esp. 21.

20. Rhode, *Justice and Gender*, 83; cf. also Carol Smart, *Feminism and the Power of Law* (London: Routledge, 1989), 75–82, 120–2, 133–7.

21. Rhode, *Justice and Gender*, 4 and passim. Rhode does not distinguish between the accommodation and acceptance perspectives within what she terms the 'disadvantage framework'.

22. Scales, 'Towards a Feminist Jurisprudence', 435. Scales abandons accommodationism in favor of MacKinnon's dominance perspective in 'The Emergence of Feminist Jurisprudence: An Essay', *Yale Law Journal* 95 (1986), 1373–403.

23. Law, 'Rethinking Sex and the Constitution', 1031.

24. Herma Hill Kay, 'Equality and Difference: The Case of Pregnancy', *Berkeley Women's Law Journal* 1 (1985), 1–38; idem, 'Models of Equality', 39–88. Kay also applies episodic analysis in the family context, where she uses it to address the social consequences of reproductive difference; see her 'Equality and Difference: A Perspective on No-fault Divorce and Its Aftermath', *University of Cincinnati Law Review* 56 (1987), 1–90. It may be that Kay's position fits more easily within the acceptance category, discussed below.

25. Littleton suggests the Supreme Court used an acceptance rather than accommodation analysis; see her 'Reconstructing Sexual Equality', 1299. See also Minow, *Making All the Difference*, 58–9, 87–8.

26. Christine A. Littleton, 'Equality across Difference: A Place for Rights Discourse?', *Wisconsin Women's Law Journal* 3 (1987), 189–212, esp. 193. Littleton earlier termed her approach 'affirmation', but withdrew the term as too celebratory; Littleton, 'Reconstructing Sexual Equality', 1297, n. 99.

27. Littleton, 'Reconstructing Sexual Equality', 1313.

28. Ibid., 1329–30.

29. Finley, 'Transcending Equality Theory', 1181–2.

30. Littleton, 'Reconstructing Sexual Equality', 1330–1.

31. Barbara A. Brown, Thomas I. Emerson, Gail Falk and Ann E. Freedman, 'The Equal Rights Amendment: A Constitutional Basis for Equal Rights for Women', *Yale Law Journal* 80 (1971), 871–985, esp. 894.

32. Law, 'Rethinking Sex and the Constitution', 975–7, 1009, n. 204.

33. Minow, *Making All the Difference*, chaps 4, 5.

34. I am here focusing on what sociologist Michele Barrett distinguishes as experiential diversity in 'The Concept of "Difference"', *Feminist Review* 26 (1987), 28–41.

35. For critiques of Gilligan's influence on feminist legal scholarship, see Kathleen Daly, 'Criminal Justice Ideologies and Practices in Different Voices: Some Feminist Questions about Justice', *International Journal of the Sociology of Law* 17 (1989), 1–18, and Joan C. Williams, 'Deconstructing Gender', *Michigan Law Review* 87 (1989), 797–845. On MacKinnon, see Angela P. Harris, 'Race and Essen-

tialism in Feminist Legal Theory', in *Feminist Legal Theory: Readings in Law and Gender*, ed. Katharine T. Bartlett and Rosanne Kennedy (Boulder, CO: Westview Press, 1991), 235–62.

36. Patricia Hill Collins argues that Black feminist thought has a several-century history; see her *Black Feminist Thought: Knowledge, Consciousness, and the Politics of Empowerment* (Boston, MA: Unwin Hyman, 1990).

37. Frances M. Beal, 'Double Jeopardy: To Be Black and Female', *New Generation* 51 (1969), 23–28 and *Sisterhood Is Powerful: An Anthology of Writings from the Women's Liberation Movement*, ed. Robin Morgan (New York: Vintage Books, 1970), 340–53.

38. For early critiques of the parallelism of the additive model, mostly but not entirely by women of color, see, for example, Elizabeth M. Almquist, 'Untangling the Effects of Race and Sex: The Disadvantaged Status of Black Women', *Social Science Quarterly* 56 (1975), 129–42; Hazel Carby, 'White Women Listen! Black Feminism and the Boundaries of Sisterhood', in *The Empire Strikes Back: Race and Racism in 70s Britain*, ed. Centre for Contemporary Cultural Studies (London: Hutchinson, 1982), 212–35; Gloria Joseph, 'The Incompatible Menage à Trois: Marxism, Feminism, and Racism', in *Women and Revolution: A Discussion of the Unhappy Marriage of Marxism and Feminism*, ed. Lydia Sargent (Boston, MA: South End Press, 1981), 91–108; Margaret A. Simons, 'Racism and Feminism: A Schism in the Sisterhood', *Feminist Studies* 5 (1979), 384–401; Elizabeth V. Spelman, 'Theories of Race and Gender: The Erasure of Black Women', *Quest* 5 (1982), 36–62; Lise Vogel, 'Correspondence: Two Views of "The Class Roots of Feminism"', *Monthly Review* 28, no. 9 (February 1977), 52–60.

39. Alice Echols, *Daring to Be Bad: Radical Feminism in America 1967–1975* (Minneapolis: University of Minnesota Press, 1989).

40. Deborah K. King, 'Multiple Jeopardy, Multiple Consciousness: The Context of a Black Feminist Ideology', *Signs* 14 (Autumn 1988), 42–72; Aida Hurtado, 'Relating to Privilege: Seduction and Rejection in the Subordination of White Women and Women of Color', *Signs* 14 (Summer 1989), 833–55; Karen Brodkin Sacks, 'Toward a Unified Theory of Class, Race, and Gender', *American Ethnologist* 16 (1989): 534–50; Collins, *Black Feminist Thought*.

41. For example, see Elsa Barkley Brown, ' "What Has Happened Here": The Politics of Difference in Women's History and Feminist Politics', *Feminist Studies* 18 (1992), 295–312; Evelyn Brooks Higginbotham, 'African-American Women's History and the Metalanguage of Race', *Signs* 17 (Winter 1992), 251–74; Chandra Talpede Mohanty, Ann Russo and Lourdes Torres, eds, *Third World Women and the Politics of Feminism* (Bloomington: Indiana University Press, 1991); Gloria Anzaldúa, ed., *Making Face, Making Soul/Haciendo Caras: Creative and Critical Perspectives by Women of Color* (San Francisco, CA: Aunt Lute Foundation Books, 1990).

42. For a bibliographical overview of socialist-feminist theory, see Lise Vogel, 'Feminist Scholarship: The Impact of Marxism', in *The Left Academy*, ed. Bertell Ollman and Edward Vernoff, vol. 3 (New York: Praeger, 1986), 1–34. For more recent discussion, see Karen V. Hansen and Ilene J. Philipson, eds, *Women, Class, and the Feminist Imagination: A Socialist-Feminist Reader* (Philadelphia: Temple University Press, 1990); and Norma Stoltz Chinchilla and Martha E. Gimenez, eds, 'Marxist-Feminist Theory', special issue of *Gender & Society* 5, no. 3 (1991).

43. Jane Gallop, Marianne Hirsch and Nancy K. Miller, 'Criticizing Feminist Criticism', in *Conflicts in Feminism*, ed. Marianne Hirsch and Evelyn Fox Keller (New York: Routledge, 1990), 349–69, esp. 363.

44. Gerda Lerner, 'Reconceptualizing Differences among Women', *Journal of Women's History* 1 (1990), 106–22; Dorothy O. Helly and Susan M. Reverby, 'Introduction: Converging on History', in *Gendered Domains: Rethinking Public and Private in Women's History*, ed. Dorothy O. Helly and Susan M. Reverby (Ithaca, NY: Cornell University Press, 1992), 1–24. See also Chapter 8 above.

45. Linda Gordon, 'The New Feminist Scholarship on the Welfare State', in *Women, the State, and Welfare*, ed. Linda Gordon (Madison: University of Wisconsin Press, 1990), 9–35, esp. 30. Hazel V. Carby, 'The Politics of Difference', *Ms Magazine* September–October 1990, 84–5; idem, 'The Multicultural Wars', *Radical History Review* 54 (1992), 7–18. See also Linda Gordon, 'On "Difference"', *Genders* 10 (1991), 91–111; and the commentaries by Sue Lees, Caroline Ramazanoglu, Kum-Kum Bhavani and Margaret Coulson on Michele Barrett and Mary McIntosh, 'Ethnocentrism and Socialist-Feminist Theory', *Feminist Review* 20 (1985), 23–47, in *Feminist Review* 22 and 23.

46. For discussion of the problem of groups see Iris Marion Young, *Justice and the Politics of Difference* (Princeton, NJ: Princeton University Press, 1990), chap. 2.

47. Minow, *Making All the Difference*.

48. Versions of this chapter were presented at the annual meetings of the American Sociological Association in 1991 and the Feminism and Legal Theory Workshop at Columbia University, New York City, in 1993. For comments I am grateful to the audiences at these presentations as well as to Kathleen Daly, Paul Montagna, Susan Reverby and Mark Tushnet.

Chapter 10: Considering Difference: The Case of the Family and Medical Leave Act of 1993

1. For feminist questioning of equality, see Chapter 9 above.
2. As detailed below, the FMLA actually offers leave to both male and

female employees who need time to care for family members or to recover from their own serious health problem.

3. S.A. Smirnov, 'Maternity Protection: National Law and Practice in Selected European Countries', *International Social Security Review* 32 (1979), 420–44; Susanne A. Stoiber, *Parental Leave and 'Woman's Place': The Implications and Impact of Three European Approaches to Family Leave Policy* (Washington, DC: Women's Research and Education Institute, 1989).

4. Adam Clymer, 'Congress Passes Measure Providing Emergency Leaves', *New York Times*, 5 February 1993, sec. A, p. 14.

5. Wendy Chavkin, 'Walking a Tightrope: Pregnancy, Parenting, and Work', in *Double Exposure: Women's Health Hazards on the Job and at Home*, ed. Wendy Chavkin (New York: Monthly Review Press, 1984), 196–213, esp. 202.

6. Alice Kessler-Harris quoted in Carol Lee Bacchi, *Same Difference: Feminism and Sexual Difference* (Sydney: Allen and Unwin, 1990), 119; Martha Minow, 'Adjudicating Difference: Conflicts among Feminist Lawyers', in *Conflicts in Feminism*, ed. Marianne Hirsch and Evelyn Fox Keller (New York: Routledge, 1990), 149–63, esp. 155.

7. A third feminist charge against the FMLA suggests it risks triggering discrimination by employers against women of childbearing age. Unlike the two critiques considered here, this charge originates in the mainstream feminist community, which is wary of any policy that can be perceived to single women out and treat them in a special manner.

8. For a sampling of this literature, see Anne Phillips, ed., *Feminism and Equality* (New York: New York University Press, 1987); Elizabeth Meehan and Selma Sevenhuijsen, eds, *Equality Politics and Gender* (London: Sage, 1991).

9. Herma Hill Kay, 'Equality and Difference: The Case of Pregnancy', *Berkeley Women's Law Journal* 1 (1985), 1–38; Lise Vogel, 'Debating Difference: Feminism, Pregnancy, and the Workplace', *Feminist Studies* 16 (1990): 9–32.

10. Lise Vogel, *Mothers on the Job: Maternity Policy in the US Workplace* (New Brunswick, NJ: Rutgers University Press, 1993).

11. Ibid.

12. I am grateful to Eloise Buker for suggesting that I make this distinction.

13. Those who pose such choices do not always make clear what they mean by maternity leave. The term traditionally refers to leave taken by biological mothers during pregnancy, for childbirth, and to care for infants and young children. In the late twentieth-century US policy context, maternity leave has been differentiated into a combination of pregnancy disability leave and parental leave.

14. Charlotte Bunch, *Passionate Politics: Feminist Theory in Action* (New York: St Martin's Press, 1987); Carol Smart, *Feminism and the Power of Law* (London: Routledge, 1989).

15. Kay, 'Equality and Difference', 12, n. 69.
16. US Congress, House, Subcommittee on Labor-Management Relations and Subcommittee on Labor Standards of the Committee on Education and Labor, *The Family and Medical Leave Act of 1987*, 100th Congress, 1st session, 25 February and 5 March 1987, 219.
17. Donna R. Lenhoff and Sylvia M. Becker, 'Family and Medical Leave Legislation in the States: Toward a Comprehensive Approach', *Harvard Journal on Legislation* 26 (1989), 403–63.
18. Institute for Women's Policy Research, *Research-in-brief: What Is Temporary Disability Insurance?* (Washington, DC: IWPR, n.d. [1993]).

INDEX

academia, 4, 19, 42, 43, 44,
101–10, 124–5
author's experience in, 8–10,
11–12, 13–14, 17
acceptance perspective, 119–20,
121
accommodation perspective, 119,
121–2
African–American women, *see*
Black women
Althusser, Louis, 98
androgyny, 115–16, 121, 131–2,
133
anthropologists, 62, 67; *see also*
Morgan, Lewis H.
assimilationism, 114–15, 116, 121,
129, 131–2, 133

Beal, Frances, 105, 123
Bebel, August, 26–7, 29, 32, 34, 67
Benston, Margaret, 54–6, 57, 59
Berkshire Conferences on the
History of Women, 100, 102,
103, 105
Black women, 45, 94, 96, 110,
123; *see also* women of color
Brenner, Johanna, 83, 85, 87,
88–9
Bridges, Amy, 25, 50
Brown, Elsa Barkley, 101
Buhle, Mari Jo, 104, 108

Carby, Hazel, 125
Chavkin, Wendy, 129
childbearing, 59; *see also* maternity
leave; pregnancy
civil rights movement, 1, 2, 10, 15,

17–18, 111; author's participation in, 6, 10–11, 14–16, 17–18,
111
class, 14–15, 29–30, 94–5, 109;
see also class struggle; sex, class
and race, linking of; working-
class women
class struggle, 33, 35–6, 37, 61,
86, 95
Collins, Patricia Hill, 124

Dalla Costa, Mariarosa, 56–7, 59
de Beauvoir, Simone, 52
democratic rights, 32, 33, 76–7,
87–8; *see also* equality
difference, 108, 110, 122; *see also*
equality versus difference debate
differential consideration, 128,
132, 134, 136
diversity, 2, 19, 110, 123–7, 136;
as means of cooptation, 19,
110, 125–6
division of labor, 73, 78–9, 81
domestic labor, 31–2, 86; Marxism
and, 31–2, 36, 37, 54–9, 75–6;
socialist feminist discussions of,
31, 43, 54–60, 64
dominance perspective, 118
dualism, 66; as a weakness in
socialist feminist theory, 62–3,
66–7, 80, 81, 85, 124
dual-systems perspective, 62–3,
85, 124, 141 n1; *see also*
dualism; family argument
DuBois, Ellen, 104, 108

Eastman, Crystal, 89

159